To: Mike

GO M.A.D.

MAKE A DIFFERENCE

Thank you for the opportunity, your amazing. Keep it going, until next time!!

— #42

Real Stuff
Real Teens Can
Do to Make a
Real Difference
...in an Unreal
World

C. Kevin Wanzer – Eric Chester – Mike Patrick
Mark Bernstein – Patty Hendrickson – Ed Gerety
Byron V. Garrett – Stu Saunders – Keith Hawkins
Chris Bowers – Willie Jolley – Ryan Underwood
Aaron Foster – Ray Lozano – Michael Scott Karpovich

Real Stuff Real Teens Can Do to
Make a Real Difference…in an Unreal World

Compiled by
Eric Chester

Published by:
ChesPress Publications
Lakewood, Colorado

Printed in the United States of America.

Cover design: Gary Gomez, Image Is Communications, Arvada, CO
Inside layout: Ad Graphics, Inc., Tulsa, OK

ISBN: 0-9651447-9-8

Go M.A.D.™
TEEN POWER and BEYOND™
TEEN POWER Thru CHRIST™
TEEN POWER™
TEEN POWER Too™
PreTEEN POWER™
TEEN EmPOWER™
LEAD NOW or Step Aside!™
are registered trademarks of Ches Press Publicatons

Published by:
ChesPress Publications
a subsidiary of Chester Performance Systems
1410 Vance St., Suite 201
Lakewood, CO 80214
(303) 239-9999

Additional copies of Go M.A.D.
can be obtained from any of the authors.
Contact information is at the end of each chapter.

Quantity discounts are available.

Web Site: www.ericchester.com

Table of Contents

Dedication

Most authors dedicate books to friends, colleagues and family members. However, the Go M.A.D. authorship team dedicates this book to you, the awesome youth of the new millennium.

You are our future. Yet, we know you have inherited a crazy, sometimes 'mad' world! You could quietly accept it as is. You could turn your back on the problems. Instead, we have noticed you joining hearts and hands, rolling up your sleeves and working together to create solutions.

You motivate us – the "professional motivators." When we visit your schools and conferences, we see the amazing talent you have. We stand in awe of the drive, the focus and the willingness you possess to make this world a better place.

Here's to you, tomorrow's leaders. We salute and applaud you and your uncompromising efforts to Go Make A Difference!

The Go M.A.D. Authorship Team

Introduction

As they go along in life, a lot of people evolve from "Pick me! Pick me! Pick me!" to "One, Two, Three…NOT IT!" From wanting to do anything to be picked, to wanting to avoid being 'it' at any cost.

What happens? Why do excited, playful children often lose their spark as they grow older – and with it – the desire to reach out to others and get involved?

Perhaps it's a failure or a feeling of insignificance that causes so many people to give up and retreat to their own private world. Deep inside every mature person is a child yearning to get out, interact with others, and make this world a better place. But fearing that their good intentions and resulting efforts will all be in vain, many tend to keep their inner child a captive prisoner. When this happens, the world feels the weight of one more taker and the loss of one less giver. What a waste.

Naturally, you are not going to let this happen to you. That is exactly why you are reading this book, and it is exactly why *we* have written it. *We* are a team of individual speakers and authors who work extensively with youth. Although our respective messages are different and unique, we are united in our belief in you, and we are all committed to empowering you to **GO M**ake **A D**ifference.

As you venture out to positively impact the people and places around you, let our words guide you and reinforce the creative and authentic path on which you walk. As you do, we are confident that you will fill the pages of your life with love and passion…hope and faith…and that we will all be better off because of you.

This book will make you think. It will cause you to look at the world differently. It will inspire you to inspire others and it will start your brain ticking with an entire section of **GO MAD**dening ideas; REAL stuff that will tell you how to make a REAL difference in this unREAL world! In short, this book is enough to make you want to **GO MAD**!

That is exactly what we have in mind.

C. KEVIN WANZER

The Best Is Not Yet to Come

CHAPTER

1

The Best Is Not Yet to Come

C. Kevin Wanzer

One of my fondest memories as a little kid was a Little Golden Book about Grover from Sesame Street. It was titled, *The Monster at the End of the Book.* Right off the bat, you knew how the story was going to end. There was going to be a monster at the end of the book. But you read the book anyway, as poor little Grover pleaded with you to stop. He would tie pages together, build brick walls and beg you to *puh-lease not* turn the pages. For each turn of the page brought you – and Grover – closer to the inevitable…*the end of the book.* And everyone knew what was waiting there…the monster.

Sure enough, the last page was one flip away and do you remember who was there waiting? Little ole' Grover was waiting in the dark. *He* was the monster at the end of the book. He was so scared of discovering himself, he did everything in his power to recruit you as an ally *not* to turn the pages. But you held his hand and together you turned page after page only to help Grover realize that the only thing he had to fear was facing his true self. You helped Grover find and rediscover himself.

There is no monster at the end of this book. As a matter of fact, there is no great surprise. Instead, this book will hold your hand as you turn the pages…helping you cut the ropes and chains that tie you down and help you regain and rediscover your authenticity…your true self.

Notice I said *rediscover.* Truth is, you already have all the answers you will ever need in your book of life. And since there is no instruction manual to life, the challenge of this chapter is to create your own. To do so, you must look within and be your own role model…your own author. You must carefully choose how to compose the pages of your life.

You have a finite number of moments just waiting for you to celebrate …to turn their pages. How you spend these moments…what you put on your pages…is totally up to you. At the end of each day, like it or not, a page in your life is turned, never to be read again. All you can take from the page is its memory. The key is how do you spend your life moments…turning pages. Do you turn them in fear, scared to death of what is around the corner…or do you fill each page with adventure and love and gratitude.

The wonderful gift of life is that with each new day, a blank page is given to us. A canvas of a page to fill with anything we want. There is not a promise for a new page tomorrow – a new day – for all we have is now. The best is not yet to come…because today is the future we have been waiting on. No day but today.

What do you fill your pages with? Some people's pages are filled with adventure, and color and faith…while others are left blank, or are dark, or are tattered and torn and mutilated. For others, their pages are the same day after day after day after day after…

I am not asking you to live your life as if today were your last day on earth. Otherwise, there would be quite a few bankrupt bank accounts and even more bankrupt souls. What I am challenging you to do is to fill the pages to the very edges and beyond. Utilize every color in your paint box of life and color your life. And never be afraid to erase and start all over. Never.

At times, it is hard to understand that now is all that really matters. We get so caught up in the destination, we don't enjoy the journey day to day. It seems, at times, we are so busy working to become someone that we are not…we forget who we are to begin with.

Some people claim that they want to live in the moment… but they cannot wait for tomorrow to get here. Eventually, tomorrow will be here and you will not be. Period. End of story…literally. What if your life ended now…if you knew today was your last…what would you wish you had done differently? What have you learned that you would share with others you love? What are things you wish you could unlearn?

To truly know yourself and relearn who you really are…you must first be willing to unlearn and shed away what you think you already know.

It is similar to the differences between that of a caterpillar and a butterfly. If you were to come from some distant planet and look at the two, you would swear they are totally separate insects. But in reality they are the same. It is just that one is more evolved than the other.

It is as if the first stage of your life is spent as a caterpillar. You learn to crawl. You absorb and actually *become* your surroundings. Life is miraculous and wonderful and you know life from a very limited point of view. Special adults nurture you and love you…and they want what is best. They tell you about *their* world and how wonderful it will be when you will be able to soar on your own. But you cannot imagine flying because everything you know tells you that you cannot fly.

You continue to grow…and wonder…and learn. Suddenly, you become still. You reflect. Perhaps, you rebel. You create a cocoon around you and you acknowledge that what you really know is that you know nothing. Suddenly, a transformation takes place. The earlier this happens in one's life, the better.

As a caterpillar, you slowly change and relearn things on your own and rediscover who you really are. Eventually, you have your very own wings. You can fly. You soar for the rest of your life amazed at this wonderful new feeling of who you really are and you will forget what it was like to crawl.

Butterflies do not regret the time spent as a caterpillar…or time in the cocoon. Butterflies relish in the moment of their newfound life…in today…thankful that their life journey has allowed them to soar to heights they could never imagine.

The sad reality is some people crawl for a very long time as a caterpillar. Some resign to the idea that life will never change. Others simply become too comfortable in their cocoons and fall asleep. They become stuck…they accept everything they have been taught as the truth and they are sentenced to a life of prejudice, apathy and routine. They sleepwalk through life. The key in truly experiencing life is to make sure not to fall back asleep and miss your life.

"The breeze at dawn has secrets to tell you.
Don't go back to sleep.
You must ask for what you really want.
Don't go back to sleep.
People are going back and forth
across the doorsill where the two worlds touch.
The door is round and open.
Don't go back to sleep."

- Rumi

The secret to being awake and alive and breaking out of your cocoon is to invest in your *uneducation.* Learn and experience life for yourself. Challenge what you have been taught. Carefully examine what and who you have been molded to become. Hold onto what you believe is authentically you, and have the strength to shed the things that you know are inconsistent to your being. Have the power to acknowledge the lies and make the choice to eliminate and correct the false truths. Prejudice, stereotypes, material possessions are all based in false truths. Acknowledge what is real…for you.

Caterpillar Myths

As children, we are told hundreds of things from well meaning adults that are not necessarily true…

- *Sticks and stones can break your bones, but words can never hurt you.*

Of course we know now that words can actually hurt more than sticks and stones. Bruises of the skin fade away…but the scars of any prejudice comment or slur – toward people from all walks of life – can last a lifetime. The key to really making a difference in ending prejudice is to take a stand for others unlike you. If someone makes a derogatory comment or joke, let him or her know how you feel in a non-confrontational way. Slowly attitudes will change…one person at a time.

- *Anything is possible.*

Well, not really. I guarantee you I will never give birth to a platypus on the face of the moon wearing a pink studded bathing suit because I removed those studs a long time ago. So, that is simply not possible, now is it? However, anything that is a true possibility is possible. ANYTHING. Pause for a moment and think of three things – that are true possibilities – which you would like to achieve. Write down one thing you would like to accomplish within the next year…one thing within the next month and one within the next week. Keep that list with you always and when you achieve one of your goals, write down a new one. Today, take one step toward one of your goals.

• *The best is yet to come.*

Life ticks by so fast. In the blink of an eye, hours, days, weeks and before you know it, a lifetime passes you by. The key to enjoying and relishing life is not focusing on how wonderful the future will be, but instead embracing this moment for what it is…a moment in life to relish and savor and embrace. To realize that this moment is the future for which we have been waiting.

Butterfly Truths

The truth is that you have to know where you have been to understand where you are now. Life is a continuous evolution…but it does not have to be spent in the cocoon, waiting to fly. I believe there are many important lessons to help you fly. Eventually we all evolve. The choice to soar is yours.

• *Break the mold. If it ain't broke, break it.*

Start by silencing your inner-critic. Children laugh and love and relish in their own being because they know no boundaries. They have no shame. They are perfect in their own imperfections. As we grow, we ironically stop growing by allowing our inner-critic to make excuses and become someone that we are not. Stop telling yourself that it is too late…that doing something that you love for a living is impractical…that people will think your nuts for trying something extraordinary. Have the courage to be you-nique and break the mold.

• *Live with an attitude of gratitude.*

Identify those in your life who really make a difference in molding who you are becoming and take the time to actually thank them. Pick up the phone...write them a letter...go visit them eye-to-eye and let them know what they mean to you.

• *Acknowledge synchronicity.*

I do not believe in coincidences. I believe that there are messages in everything that surrounds us. The universe is always speaking loud and clear. It is our job to interpret and recognize what is being said. A certain song on the radio just when you need to hear it...a friend calling just when you need them...a butterfly landing on your shoulder. Messages surround us. Be open to listening...and receiving.

• *Simplify, simplify, simplify.*

Hold onto memories...not stuff.

• *Grow up to be a child.*

You are a child. You always will be for the rest of your life. Look at the world through those eyes...with wonder and curiosity and love. If you live as a child, you will love as a child. A child does not live for the future. A child is totally in the moment, relishing in whatever this day holds...making the most of it and learning from the past. Allow yourself time to take a recess from life. To engage in activities that feed your soul. Write. Paint. Sing. Dance. Live life fully.

• *Be your word.*

Make a commitment to yourself that your word actually means something. Commit to keeping promises, being on time and living a life of integrity.

Take a risk to unlearn certain things you have been taught. Unlearn that life is unfair…that prejudice is acceptable… that the good guys always finish last. Make a conscious choice to LIVE your life. After all, life is a choice. To truly choose to live is to choose to Make A Difference. Starting today…make a choice to GO M.A.D.

Volunteer at a retirement community to play cards with residents…start a mentoring program of older students working with younger ones…get involved with a public service group…read to the blind…donate time to those in need…raise money for a charity walk…whatever it is, GO M.A.D.

We all walk together on a common ground each composing our own manuscripts. Today is a new page in your book of life. What will you possibly create? What lessons will you take with you and are you able to understand that this is the moment you have been waiting for? Understand that the best is not yet to come because tomorrow is only a promise…with no guarantees.

Here we are at the end of the chapter and we discovered that there is nothing to fear. Grover would be so proud. Heck, we can learn a lot from Grover. Be furry. Be funny. Be lov-able. Travel near…and far. And that sometimes the only thing we have to fear is exactly what we should embrace…being ourselves.

If you do this, you are sure to live,
happily ever laughter…

ABOUT THE AUTHOR

C. Kevin Wanzer

Since 1983, as a sophomore in high school, Kevin Wanzer has been known to "reach the unreachable" with his hilarious "Got ALOHA?" message. He has literally lost count of the hundreds of conferences, thousands of schools and millions of audience members that have laughed and learned with Kevin. Few words can describe his electrifying assembly that is touching, fast-paced and down right outrageous. Whether it be in elementary cafe-gym-aterias…middle or high school auditoriums...colleges and Universities...or the plethora of state-wide and national youth and adult leadership conferences he has addressed in North America and beyond, every individual leaves Kevin's program with a challenge to grow up to be a child and with a renewed sense to impact the lives of others in a positive way. Kevin lives in Indianapolis and dedicates his chapter to his angels Hannah, Anna and Angelina and his soul companion Brandon, along with Dreifus – the three-legged dog.

Got Aloha?
Post Office Box 30384
Indianapolis, IN 46230-0384
317-253-4242 Fax: 317-475-0956
Toll Free: 1-800-4-KEVIN-W
Email: GoMAD@KevinWanzer.com
Web Sites: www.GotAloha.org or www.KevinWanzer.com

ERIC CHESTER

Rise and Tell

Why, When and How to R.A.T.

CHAPTER

2

Rise and Tell

Why, When and How to R.A.T.

Eric Chester

Snitch. Fink. Nark. Rat.

Face it. No one likes a tattletale. There is an unspoken code among friends – and even among foes – that telling on another's wrongdoing is taboo, even bad luck. To earn peer acceptance and your merit badge of "cool," you've to got to look the other way, keep your mouth shut and *take it to the grave!*

Or do you?

Let's say someone ripped you off or talked smack behind your back. If a third party confided who dunnit, would you call them a rat – or a person of integrity who showed courage in speaking up about the injustice?

Funny how the labels change when the roles are reversed, isn't it?

The point is that right is right and wrong is wrong, and there is no right way to do a wrong thing. However, society's code of silence makes it possible – at times even simple –

for wrong to overcome what's right. When that happens, all too often innocent people get hurt while guilty people go on doing bad stuff.

Still, sticking your nose where it doesn't belong could come back and bite you on the butt, right? It's so much easier, safer and even cooler to pretend you never knew what went down.

Only you do know, and if you ignore an opportunity to right a wrong, you enable the wrong and cripple the right. Sometimes, making a positive difference will challenge you to R.A.T. – to **R**ise **A**nd **T**ell.

To R.A.T or Not to R.A.T.?

Imagine that your algebra teacher has absentmindedly left the answer key to the upcoming semester final on her desk. When a minor emergency calls her away, two students dash to her desk and begin copying the key while another kid keeps a lookout by the door. Within hours, the exam answers have circulated throughout the school, and everyone seems to be taking advantage of the free information.

If you studied hard all semester and could ace the exam without the unauthorized help, would it be fair that so many others could ace it too by cheating? On the other hand, what if you were flunking algebra and needed at least a B on the final to pass the class? The study time would force you to miss a popular weekend concert, one you have a back stage pass to attend. Cheating would insure a great test score without any work.

Would you R.A.T?

If your response changed even slightly because of variations in this situation, then you've fallen victim to *situational ethics*. As mentioned earlier, there is no right way – or right reason – to do a wrong thing.

The right thing would involve telling the teacher about the answer key floating around school. You could speak to her in person or drop an anonymous note in her mailbox at the main office. However, if considerations about your own grade in any way entered into your decision to R.A.T., then you might do the right thing for the wrong reason. This is better than doing the wrong thing for any reason, but it ain't what this chapter – or this book – is about!

I'm not suggesting you become public enemy #1 by blabbing every mistake, indiscretion or misjudgment made by another. This will only cause peers to dislike you intensely and authority figures to question your credibility. That's why knowing when to R.A.T. is critical.

When to R.A.T.

Have you ever found out something you wish you never knew? That's when your conscience needs to declare war with your sense of loyalty to a friend, your fear of stepping forward, your sense of cool or perhaps all three. It would be so much easier if you just didn't know what you know. But alas, it's too late. You know!

Then what?

Before you Rise And Tell, find someone you *can* and *should* tell – a trustworthy person with the authority to appropriately deal with the situation. Your confidant could be a police officer, teacher, principal or counselor because these professionals are skilled in handling crisis situations. Don't play off of negative stereotypes that make them out to be clueless or that make you out to be a nark for seeking them. This twisted thinking allows bad things to go on happening to good people.

Remember that it's okay to remain anonymous. Make certain from the start that the authority figure you approach will protect your identity. But don't tell them something important and then ask them to do nothing.

During my teaching career, some students would say, "Mr. Chester, if I tell you something, will you promise not to tell anyone else?"

I soon figured out how dangerous that question was. If I agreed, then my hands were tied. What could I do if I learned that a student was going to beat up another kid, or that the person in front of me was contemplating suicide? Upholding that promise strictly would mean remaining silent. You've got to trust your confidant enough let them decide on the best course of action while they at the same time respect your request for privacy.

Also, before you Rise And Tell make absolutely certain that you have your facts straight. If you hear through the grapevine that something dangerous is about to go down, it's extremely important to pass on the information for what it is – rumor, not fact.

Don't hold back. Tell the authority figure everything you know – and even everything you believe. Just take pains to distinguish between the two so the adult can respond as appropriately as possible.

When not to R.A.T.

I have two children and two stepchildren. The youngest is now pushing age 18. But when I look back on when we all lived under the same roof, I'm certain they spilled only the most annoying drivel:

> "Dad! Zac chewed the ears off of my chocolate Easter Bunny!"
>
> or
>
> "Whitney snuck your new razor to shave her legs!"
>
> or
>
> "Travis peeked inside his birthday present and then re-wrapped it!"
>
> or
>
> "Holli spit her vegetables in the toilet!"

This kind of tattletale crapola drove me nuts! But the code of silence kicked in when any of my kids really screwed up. Someday when I'm 90 years old and rocking in a nursing home, one of my then-65-year-old children might visit to confess that at age 8 they knocked-off a neighborhood lemonade stand and snorted powdered sugar off donut holes by age 11. That's the stuff I really needed to know, not necessarily to discipline, but more to help guide them.

R.A.T.: The Good, the Bad and the Ugly

The Good

The notorious Enron scandal of 2002 rocked the financial world and opened the door to shameful accounting practices being conducted by other corporate giants. Although you probably didn't lose a lot of money or sleep over the fiasco, tens of thousands of good employees – and millions of innocent people – were made to suffer for the actions of a few. It's hard to imagine how the situation could have been worse, but it might have escalated still more had it not been for one very brave R.A.T.

As vice president of corporate development for Enron, Sherron Watkins discovered that the company had inflated its financial statements and falsely reported income to investors and employee stockholders. She knew that *ratting out* her company's illegal activities to the authorities could devastate her financially and even ruin her career. But she refused to look the other way. She blew the whistle and even testified against her employer in U.S. congressional hearings.

Many other Enron executives knew the company was breaking the law, but they were too afraid to come forward – too afraid that they might lose their position, their stock options or their job. Perhaps, they were too afraid that they would be considered a rat.

Yet, by acting in an unselfish and courageous way, Watkins did more than simply stop Enron's corrupt business practices. She helped shine a spotlight on other corporations engaging in similarly illegal and harmful conduct. Consequently, *Time* magazine named her its distinguished "Person of the Year for 2002" and devoted a cover story to this true R.A.T.

The Bad

Jake had it bad for Kayleen, but she was dating Ryan and had no intention of trying her luck on the free agent market. One day after soccer practice, Jake overheard Ryan tell

Trevor that he thought the new transfer student Sara was "totally hot." Two days later, he saw Ryan and Sara talking at a Dairy Queen. Pining for Kayleen, Jake drew some conclusions and passed his assumptions on as facts to Kayleen during physics class. Hurt by this gossip, Kayleen blew up at Ryan, accused him of cheating on her with Sara and then broke up with him.

Jake's mean spirited ratting victimized Ryan and Kayleen. Sure, Ryan had made flattering comments about Sara to a friend in confidence. When he ran into Sara at the local DQ, he did talk with her as they waited in line. But Ryan had done nothing to warrant Kayleen's wrath. Jake ratted with half-truths to achieve some gain by causing someone else's pain.

The Ugly

According to a variety of sources, Dylan Klebold and Eric Harris had shared some of their deadly April 20, 1999, plans for Columbine High School students and teachers. Many in the know probably wrote off the dark schemes as a tasteless joke by a couple of eerie loners. Others were sworn to secrecy. Some undoubtedly stopped short of ratting for fear of how the pair might retaliate. So the terrible Klebold and Harris secret was kept, and 13 lives were lost at the suburban Denver high school that day.

If only there had been someone bold enough to R.A.T.

Life at the Crossroads

Sometimes deciding to R.A.T. is a snap. However, more often you might need a little coaching. It's probably a good idea when:

- Someone is at risk of physical injury
- A law is broken
- Not telling means that an innocent person will needlessly suffer

By contrast, deciding to R.A.T. is a not a good idea if you just want to get someone in trouble, make yourself look good in the eyes of another or when the error made seems inconsequential.

As you might imagine, lots of middle ground stretches between the *always* and *never* extremes of R.A.T. That expansive *gray zone* demands that you rely on your sense of morality. However, because there is no end to making judgment calls, and because stress may tempt you to choose poorly, planning ahead is critical. You need to develop a personal philosophy of when you will Rise and Tell, and when you will remain silent.

Pop Quiz

Would you R.A.T. if you:

- Spotted someone shoplifting from a convenience store?
- Discovered that a neighbor was cheating on his wife?
- Noticed your little brother didn't brush his teeth, but told your Mom he did?
- Learned your cousin was hooked on Ecstasy?
- Remembered a license plate number of a car driven by someone who pumped gas, but never paid for it?

- Knew a friend's dad was beating him, but your friend begged you not to tell?
- Realized a coworker called in sick so he could go to a game?
- Heard from your best friend that she was pregnant?
- Saw a kid bringing a knife to school?
- Got threatened by a gang member?
- Spied a classmate vandalizing the car of an unpopular teacher?
- Watched a kid write 'fag' on a poster of a student running for office?
- Learned that several tough seniors were planning to give a special-ed freshman a wedgy?
- Witnessed your favorite teacher make a pass at a student?
- Caught a kid butting in the cafeteria line?
- Knew your buddy got a fake I.D. to buy beer?

No two people will agree on all of the above. Yet, some situations seem so minor that the mere thought of telling is ridiculous. That's good! Nobody likes a tattletale, and I am not suggesting that you become one.

On the other hand, many of these scenarios might have caused you to squirm with good reason. But if you attached names and faces to the characters before deciding, you may have bent your *ethics* to fit the *situation*. That makes you guilty of the *situational ethics* discussed earlier. For example, if the shoplifter was a big, bad bruiser, would you have kept your mouth shut? How much did you like the teacher whose car was being vandalized? Was the student just "asking" for the advances of your favorite teacher?

Be wary of situational ethics. It's trouble when good people decide to R.A.T. or not based on their relationship to those involved rather than on their knowledge of right and wrong. Those seeking to make a positive difference in this world should not consider personal likes and dislikes, but rather a firm set of values and principles.

The Challenge

Throughout this chapter, you may have been thinking, "Geez. If I did what this guy is suggesting and spilled my guts, if I did rat on (______________), then something really bad could happen to me! I know I should do something, and I know I could make a positive difference. But it would be so much easier to stay out of it!"

Don't be alarmed. This kind of internal dialogue only means that your conscience is working properly. Yet, that conscience may slip away if you don't pay attention.

I challenge you to listen and to find a way to do what's right. Speak up! You can always do it anonymously. Or, you may first approach the "doer" to give them the opportunity to come clean. No matter what, don't let fear or peer pressure force you to mind your own business and keep your mouth shut. Instead, do what you know needs to be done. Rise And Tell.

ABOUT THE AUTHOR

Eric Chester

For more than a decade, Eric has been preparing teenagers for the real world, and preparing the world for a new generation. His acclaimed presentations have empowered 1.5 million students, parents, educators, and business professionals worldwide. Eric is synonymous with leadership, keynoting as many as 50 large student leadership conferences each year, including the National Association of Student Councils, Key Clubs, DECA, FBLA, FFA, SADD, 4H, etc. He is the founder, co-author, and publisher for the TEEN POWER/ LEAD NOW book series, and has written a business book for managers entitled EMPLOYING GENERATION WHY. Eric and his family live atop Lookout Mountain in Golden, Colorado.

Generation Why, Inc.
1410 Vance Street – Ste. #201
Lakewood, CO 80214
303-239-9999 Fax: 303-239-9901
Toll Free: 800-304-ERIC
Email: eric@ericchester.com
Web Site: www.ericchester.com

ED GERETY

No Joke!

Bringing down Bullying...
Building up Respect

CHAPTER

3

No Joke!

Bringing down Bullying... Building up Respect

Ed Gerety

"What a loser! Look at him over there. He has the same shirt on that he's had on for the past two weeks can you believe it? How disgusting! He is such a geek." The four high school students then began to laugh out loud as they stared at the boy who was sitting by himself at the other end of their table. It was evident that the boy could hear what the other students were saying about him. He was hunched over and eating his sandwich as quickly as possible – not making eye contact with anyone.

I was sitting one table away, eating lunch with a group of students, and observed this boy being picked on. Quickly, I stood up and walked over to the four students because I knew something about that boy that they didn't know. It was something that the principal of their high school had shared with me earlier that morning.

"Excuse me," I said to the four students, "could I please speak to all of you outside in the hallway for a moment?"

One of the girls looked up at me from where she was sitting and gave me the look – the kind of look to let someone know that you think they don't belong. A look that can tear someone down and make them feel small.

In an irritated and arrogant voice she said, "Who are you?" Her friend next to her said, "Yeaaaah, who are you?"

"My name is Ed; I'm just a guest here. Could I please speak to the four of you out in the hallway?" I asked again. One of the guys in the group became annoyed by my request and said, "Yo, can you just talk to us right here? Our lunch is pretty quick – it's like five seconds." I said no and asked a third time for them to step out into the hallway with me.

Reluctantly, the four students got up and followed me out. They began to mumble to one another, "You've got to be kidding me, this is ridiculous. Yeah, this is such a joke."

The four students stood against the wall with their arms folded. All of them were now giving me the look of disapproval.

"Why were you making fun of that boy sitting at your table?" I asked.

One of the girls stepped forward and said, "We weren't making fun of anybody. What is your problem?" And her friend said, "Yeaaaah, what is your problem?"

"Do you know anything about the boy that you were laughing at a moment ago?"

One of the guys then took a step forward to get into my face and smiled at his friends as he did it. He was the tough guy of the group and probably acted this way to try to impress his friends. He said, "Yeah, what's the big deal? You got a problem with that?"

"Do you want to know why he probably has had the same shirt on for the past two weeks?"

He answered, "I don't know man, because he's a loser!"

The four students burst out laughing.

"Do you know where he's been going for the past two weeks?" I asked. "About a half an hour before school gets out, his mother picks him up in front of the school. They drive an hour to the children's hospital to see his younger brother. His younger brother is going through a bone marrow transplant. The boy spends the night next to him in the hospital. His younger brother is scared, they are best friends, and it's the only brother he's got. Did you know that?"

The four students looked at me with surprise and embarrassment. All they could say was, "We didn't know. Yeah, we didn't know, uh, we didn't know."

"How were you supposed to know?" This was the last question I asked. The students had nothing more to say and just walked quietly back into the cafeteria to finish their lunch.

As I went back into the cafeteria I looked for the boy they had been making fun of but the boy – was gone.

What do you think the boy was feeling as he was being made fun of, picked on, and bullied? Do you wonder if he felt all alone or if he had anyone to talk to? It doesn't matter what grade you are in or how old you are, it's easy to remember a time when you were picked on – it's not hard to forget.

How do your classmates, friends, or teammates feel when they've been picked on, teased, had a rumor spread about them, an email written about them, or bullied? The next time you go to make fun of someone – stop; remind yourself that you do not know everything about anyone. You may know what clothes a person wears, what sports they play, what car they drive, and who they are dating. But we don't know everything about them.

Do you know what happened to them this morning before they came to school? Do you know when they wake up in the morning they pass their mother in the kitchen, they don't look or speak to each other, and it's been going on this way for six months? You know that person that you're giving a hard time to – do you know that they are dealing with a drug addiction? An eating disorder? Do you know that their girlfriend is pregnant? Or that they are pregnant? Do you know where they lived before they moved to your town?

We don't know everyone's story. The challenge we have is to be respectful, sensitive, and compassionate, not only to the people that we know, but also to the people and the things that we do not know everything about.

People will sometimes justify that if they know the person they are making fun of, or if they are friends with the person they are picking on, it's ok to tease or give them a hard time. It still hurts – sometimes even more. For instance, your best friend comes to school and she is wearing a new jacket. To get a cheap laugh from all your friends you decide to make a comment such as, "Nice jacket who are you trying to be, a MTV super star?" All your friends laugh at your comment and so does your best friend you just picked on! She doesn't want you to know that what you said really hurt her. What you don't notice is that she never wears that jacket again. Or maybe it's when you're hanging out with your buddy who's not as skinny as you are and you poke fun at his shape and size. Then everyone around you laughs including your buddy. What you don't know is that inside it has really hurt him to hear what you've said.

Our words and our actions will always do one of two things: they will either tear people down or build people up. Ultimately, this is at the heart of making a difference in your school, community, and the world. Even knowing this, the bullying and teasing continues to the point where it's enough to make you Go M.A.D.!

The following challenges provide an opportunity for you to be someone who creates an environment of respect and appreciation for all people. If you accept these challenges then you will be someone who is truly taking action and making a real difference.

Challenge #1: Respect Day

Create a respect day at your school. Invite the teachers and students from your school to wear a ribbon (in your school colors) to symbolize respect for yourself and one another. This will create an awareness of the importance of respect. Hang posters throughout your school that have powerful messages or quotes about respect, character, and kindness. Create one big poster or banner where each person can trace their hand in various colored markers and sign their name around a saying of your choice such as 'united we stand' or 'respect for yourself and one another' signifying each person's commitment to being respectful of one another. Contact your local newspaper and invite them to write a story about your day.

Challenge #2: Helping Hands

Develop three 10-minute skits and/or role plays about respect, character, and kindness. Include the issues and effects of bullying, teasing, and gossip. Perform these skits for the middle or elementary school students in your town. Allow time for a question and answer session with the students. In doing this project you and your peers will be serving as positive role models and helping other students learn about these issues.

Challenge #3: Caring Cards

Gather a list of local and national hotline numbers that specialize in the issues students at your school may be facing. For example: drug and alcohol abuse, eating disorders, violence, and depression. Print these numbers on one side of a business card. On the other side of the card print an inspirational quote or saying of your choice. Distribute the caring cards to each student at your school during homeroom or at an all school event.

Challenge #4: You've Got A Friend

Find someone who is sitting alone during lunch and ask them if you and your friend can join them. In a conversation with this person try to learn three things that you have in common with them. Who knows? You may make a new friend!

Challenge #5: Bully Free Zone

Design and create a poster for the entrance of your school to indicate that your school is a bully free zone. The purpose of the bully free zone is to promote an environment of respect and appreciation for all people. Model the concept of a "no smoking" sign. Make stickers of your poster design for teachers to use in their classroom. Posting this statement will create an ongoing awareness of the importance of decreasing and eliminating bullying at school.

Challenge #6: Parent-Student-Teacher Awareness Night

Host a special night at your school where parents, students, and teachers can participate in a discussion about topics such as respect, character, and kindness. Explore the questions around what causes bullying and what can be done as an individual, as a family, and as a community to stop it. Consider implementing any of the ideas that are generated from this event and celebrate the group's commitment to the issues.

Challenge #7: Tap Into Talent

Find the people at your school who are talented in the areas of art, music, hobbies, sports and more. Create a fun event for these people to showcase their talents. This will provide an opportunity for the people at your school to learn something about someone that they may not have known before. This event could celebrate the diversity and uniqueness within your school.

Challenge #8: Beyond The Classroom

Create a section in your school newspaper to highlight one or two teachers in each edition. Ask the teachers you highlight to provide some interesting facts about themselves, some unique experiences that they've had, or hobbies they enjoy. The purpose of the teacher highlights is for students to learn something about their teachers that they didn't know before. This goes beyond the classroom to create a community of respect, uniqueness, diversity, and appreciation.

Challenge #9: Make Your Mark

Design a mural that can be painted on a designated wall at your school. The mural can contain positive words and qualities such as: respect, gratitude, kindness, appreciation, belief, and more. Recruit some of the talented artists you found from challenge #7 to help with the design and painting of the mural. A mural is a powerful statement, which can be viewed by everyone on a daily basis as a reminder of the importance of respect and appreciation for all people.

Challenge #10: It's Your Choice

When you are building respect for yourself and one another you will be faced with a variety of choices and decisions. As a student leader, it is important to be aware that there are many different areas that influence the choices and decisions that you make: your friends, family, religion, attitude, the media, past experiences and so on. Choices from what we allow to be put into our bodies, to how we resolve a conflict, to our goals and dreams, even the relationships in which we get involved. Below are five powerful questions that you can ask yourself when you are about to make a difficult choice or decision:

- Is this choice consistent with what I believe in?
- Am I being influenced in a positive or negative way?
- Will this choice hurt me or another?
- Will this choice bring me closer to my goals and dreams?
- How will I feel about this choice in one week, in one month, in one year?

Write these questions down and post them in a place that you look at often such as, the inside of your locker, on your mirror at home, or in your student planner. Use them as a tool for making positive choices and decisions in your life.

The Ultimate Challenge: Walk The Talk

Lead by example. It is not only what you say, but also what you do. Your words and your actions will always do one of two things: they will either tear people down or build people up. Respect yourself. Great leaders have a respect for themselves and for one another. Know that you have the power to choose in every moment of your life and you are responsible for the consequences of your choices. No joke! You can bring down bullying by building up respect.

ABOUT THE AUTHOR

Ed Gerety

Ed is one of the top professional youth speakers and leadership trainers in the United States. His passion, humor, and ability to connect with the hearts and minds of his audience has inspired people in all 50 states, Canada, and Europe reaching over one million people and counting. His presentations focus on respect, character, appreciation, leadership, attitude, and making a difference. Ed is the author of *Combinations: Opening the Door to Student Leadership* and is a contributing author to the *Teen Power* series. He lives in Exeter, New Hampshire with his wife Suzanne.

Ed Gerety
Gerety Presentations
4 Captain's Way
Exeter, NH 03833
Fax: 603-772-5416
Toll Free: 800-207-2580
Email: ed@geretypresentations.com
Web Site: www.geretypresentations.com

Don't Make Decisions for Today!

CHAPTER

4

Don't Make Decisions for Today!

Willie Jolley

Would you like to influence your friends? Do you want to make an impact on your family and community? Do you want to do great things with your life? If the answer to these questions is YES, then read on, my friend!

A few years ago, I worked with the Washington DC Public School System as a Drug Prevention Coordinator. My job was to work with young people and show them the power they had within themselves and how they could positively impact their friends.

I developed a program called Positive Images. This was a Peer Leadership Development Program that taught young people how to positively influence their peers. It was during that year and within that school system that I learned the profound impact one young person could have! Many young people who had been going the wrong way made drastic U-turns in their lives after positive encounters with peer leaders.

During that year, I discovered that if you want to really make a difference you have to become a leader. I also learned that before you can lead others, you must first learn to lead yourself. Leaders need to make tough decisions and they must live a life of courage.

Maya Anjelou, the great poet and humanitarian wrote, *"in order to be the best you that you can be - it will take courage! You must have courage to be kind, to be helpful, to be fair and to do the right things in life!"* According to Ms. Angelou, *"it is easy to follow the crowd and do the wrong things, but it takes courage to take a stand and do the right things."*

It takes courage to say no to drugs and violence. It takes courage to tell friends who tell racist jokes that what they are doing is wrong. It takes courage to be a person of strong convictions and avoid following the crowd. It takes courage to be a leader and to be a person who is serious about making a difference.

As a kid growing up in DC, my two best friends were Michael and Anthony. The three of us first met in the 2nd grade and became instant buddies. We ate lunch together, hung out after school together, played games together and even did our homework together. In junior high school, the three of us took on a paper route delivering the Washington Times. We split the work evenly, collected the money, and after paying for our papers, split the profits between us. On Saturday mornings we'd go to the Mall to buy identical outfits because we wanted to look like brothers. The three of us were inseparable!

We started high school together, and although we remained best friends, we found ourselves going in different directions. Michael was very athletic and he wound up on the football and basketball teams. Being musical, I sang in the choir and played trumpet with the school orchestra. Anthony didn't have any special interests other than girls, so he spent most of his spare time simply hanging out with a crowd.

When it came time to graduate from high school, Michael graduated and was offered a football scholarship to Howard University. I graduated and got an intern scholarship to American University. Anthony, on the other hand, dropped out of school. He wanted to impress girls and make fast money, so Anthony began selling drugs.

Fours years went by and Michael graduated from college. He wanted to continue his education and go to law school but his parents couldn't afford to send him. They had five other children who were either in college or about to go to college, so Michael started looking for scholarships that might pay for his tuition and expenses. He called every law school in the country inquiring about scholarship help and after an exhaustive search, struck gold at the University of Illinois. The counselors there told Michael that he met the qualifications of their scholarship program, but that he would have to come immediately for a personal interview. Michael told them that he didn't have the money for transportation and that it would take him some time to earn or borrow the necessary funds. But the university told Michael if he didn't come soon, they would be forced to give the scholarship to someone else.

Michael called his parents, but they couldn't help him. He called me and every other friend he could think of, but no one had the money Michael needed. He tried to get a loan but couldn't find any bank that would lend him the money he needed to get to Illinois. So Michael did the only thing he could do to raise money. He sold his jewelry, clothes, television, CD player, his stereo, and almost everything he had to get enough money for a one-way ticket to Chicago.

When he arrived, Michael rushed to the Registrar's Office on the campus of the University of Illinois. He made his way to the front of the line and said, *"I'm Michael from Washington DC. I've been trying for weeks and I had to do a lot, but I'm finally here!"* The admission's officer looked down the roll and caught her breath as she responded. *"I am sorry, but it's too late. We gave the last slot away about four days ago. I'm sorry, but you'll have to try again next year."*

Michael was devastated. He didn't have enough money to get back home and didn't know anyone in Chicago. He rented a small room in a local boarding house and upon entering, he sat and cried. But after hours of crying, Michael realized that his tears would not change his circumstances. If he was going to turn his problem into a possibility, he had to not only have a dream; he'd have to take action on that dream!

That next morning, Michael woke up bright and early. He put on his best clothes, went to the registrar's office and said, *"Hello. I'm back and I came to find out how I can get into class."* The lady looked at him and said, *"I'm sorry I wasn't clearer yesterday, but there is no more room available. All the scholarships have been taken. You will have to try again next year.*" Michael turned and walked away and returned to his small room. The next morning, he woke up, put on his best clothes and went back to the registrar's office.

"Hello I'm back! Just checking to see if someone dropped out or changed their mind. Just trying to see how I can get into class!" The stunned lady replied, *"Sorry, but you will have to try again next year. Not this year, next year! Goodbye."* The next morning, Michael woke up early, put on his best clothes and went back to the registrar's office and said, *"Hello, I'm back to see if someone got sick or changed their mind. I want to know how I can get into class!"* He was sent away again. Yet, he continued to come back day after day.

Michael was not discouraged and kept returning to the Registrar's office every day for 20 consecutive days. On the 20th day, the Dean of the Law School heard him say, *"I'm going to keep coming back until I get into law school!"* The Dean asked Michael if he was the one who came from Washington DC that kept coming back every-day, even though he'd been told that school registration was closed. Michael admitted that he was the one, and shocked the Dean when he said that he was going to keep coming back until he was admitted. Seeing how badly Michael wanted to go to law school, the Dean offered Michael a work-study spot. He told Michael that if he was really serious, he could work his way through school. Michael replied enthusiastically, *"I'd do anything... anything to go to this law school!"*

The Dean gave Michael a job on the custodial team. His job responsibilities meant that he had to clean up after the other students. He cleaned the cafeteria, the bathrooms, even the toilets. He worked eight hours a day and attended class eight hours a day. Then every night, Michael went to study in the library for at least four hours. This meant that after work, school, and studying, Michael got a grand total of fours hours of sleep each night only to awaken and do it all over again!

Michael refused to give up. He realized that if he was going to be a lawyer, he could not just do what was comfortable. He had to do what was necessary.

While Michael was fighting his way through law school, I was singing my way through graduate school. My classes lasted from eight in the morning until about four in the afternoon. Then I would head to the recording studio to sing jingles (music to radio and television commercials) from about five until eight. After that, I would go to my job as a singer for a local nightclub where the hours were from nine until midnight. By the time I paid my rent and my tuition, there was very little money left. As a result, my dinners were usually comprised of tuna fish, or hot dogs and beans.

All this time, our friend Anthony, was rolling in the dough. He had plenty of money because he was selling drugs. He was driving around in a shiny new black Mercedes Benz. He had all the latest tennis shoes and really fancy clothes. Anthony was always surrounded by pretty girls and he was always seen at the finest restaurants. When he saw me walking from school to the studio, he would beep his horn and wave.

I vividly remember walking to work one day during the freezing cold. Anthony drove beside me, rolled down his window and asked why I was out in the cold. I told him I was walking from class. He said, "You're still in school?" I told him I had finished college and was now in graduate school and that I couldn't yet afford a car. Anthony stopped, pulled out a big wad of one hundred dollar bills – the most money I had ever seen – and said, *"Willie, we were like brothers when we were young and now I'm going to make you an offer that will make us like brothers again. If you come work with me, I'll make sure you have this kind of money and I'll get you a nice car!"*

It sounded so tempting! I was tired of walking and I was tired of being poor. I was tired of the struggles of school and work. I reached out to take the money from his hand when I heard a voice in my head that I had not heard for many years. It was the voice of my ninth grade English teacher who always told us, *"Leaders don't make decisions for today; they make their decisions for tomorrow!"*

As my hand moved closer towards the money, the voice in my head got even louder *"Leaders don't make decisions for today; they make their decisions for tomorrow!"* Just as I was about to grab the money from his hand and take him up on his offer, the voice in my head got personal, ***"Willie Jolley! Leaders don't make decisions for today; they make their decisions for tomorrow! Either live your own dreams or you will end up living someone else's dreams!"***

At that moment I pulled my hand back and said, *"Yo, Anthony. I appreciate your offer, but I have to pass. I have to live my dreams, not yours!"* Then I walked away.

Where did the three boys who were inseparable in grade school eventually end up?

Michael is a currently a professor of law at Howard University. He is also a renowned sports agent who represents many professional football players in the NFL. This past year, several of his clients were first round draft picks. The average salary for an NFL player is more than one million dollars per year of which Michael earns a nice percentage. This year, Michael will earn in excess of four million dollars!

Anthony now lives in Marion, Indiana. His room is a 6' x 8' cell with bars on the door and on the window. The last time I visited Anthony was through a thick glass wall at a jail in DC before his move to Marion. He picked up a phone on one side of the glass and I picked up a phone on the other and asked, *"How's it going?"* He replied, *"It's tough in here!" "Could you do me a favor and take my kids some Christmas presents?"* I said, *"Sure!"* He then said, *"Could you go visit my mother? She has been sick and I really miss her. Would you go visit her and give her a kiss for me?"* Of course I told him that I would. Then I asked, *"Anthony, when are you going to get out of here?"* His answer devastated me. He said, *"I won't be out of jail for fifty years!"* My childhood friend will not be out of jail until he is eighty years old! Anthony's life is wasted because he made his decisions for today – for the moment – not thinking of tomorrow!

The moral of the story?

Now is the time for you to become the best leader you can become. You've got to strive to reach your potential if you want to be able to positively impact your friends. You must have courage to stand for what is good and right, and not just what is cool or 'in' right now. Occasionally, you will have to go against the crowd; against what is popular; against what everyone else is doing; and against the tide.

Go forth and become a 'leader of self' and a then become a leader of your peers! Have the courage to make a difference by taking a stand!

Points To Remember:

You always have choices, but you can never choose the consequences of those choices!

Peer pressure can be positive or poison!

Turn problems into possibilities by dreaming.

Make your own destiny! Take a stand!

ABOUT THE AUTHOR

Willie Jolley

Willie is an award winning speaker, singer and author of two best selling books, "It Only Takes A Minute To Change Your Life," and "A Setback Is A Setup For A Comeback." In 1999, Toastmasters International chose him "Motivational Speaker Of The Year!"

Mr. Jolley has spoken to over a million youth in the last decade from – Alabama to Australia! His PBS Youth Special has become one of the top selling videos in America! Mr. Jolley focuses on empowering youth to make wise choices and becoming the leaders they were born to be!

He resides in Washington, DC with his wife and son.

Willie Jolley Worldwide
PO Box 55459
Washington, DC 20040
202-723-8863 Fax: 202-722-1180
Toll Free: 800-487-8899
Email: info@WillieJolley.com
Web Site: www.williejolley.com

MARK BERNSTEIN

Kindness: The Ultimate Selfish Act?

CHAPTER

5

Kindness: The Ultimate Selfish Act?

Mark Bernstein

Pursue your dreams.

How lame is that? Pursue your dreams? You don't know who I am and I don't know you, but I'm telling you to pursue your dreams? How often do you hear a speaker or teacher tell you to pursue your dreams when they have NO CLUE how hard your life is? And this same person probably doesn't even have enough courage to pursue his own dreams. So, I take it back. Don't pursue your dreams. Instead…

Follow your heart.

Oh man, that's even worse. Follow your heart? Suddenly I sound like a Celine Dion song. You can't just drop everything and follow your heart, can you? You have schoolwork, a job, relationship issues, family problems, stress out the wazoo and I'm telling you to follow your heart? Yeah, right, like it's that simple. Okay, I take it back. Don't follow your heart. Instead…

Seek your purpose.

Now I've turned into Obi-Wan Kenobi. *Seek your purpose, young Jedi, and don't trust anyone wearing a dark helmet with breathing problems.* I'm surprised you're still reading this chapter because I have gone completely mad. Here I am, typing at my computer. It's 5 a.m. and I haven't slept in days. I'm stressed about deadlines, I have a cold that will not go away, and my cats won't stop throwing up on the living room carpet. Plus, I have a fever blister on my upper lip that's about the size of a loaf of bread. Seriously, it's like a giant piece of French toast glued to my lips. And **I**, of all people, have the nerve to tell **YOU** to pursue your dreams, follow your heart and seek your purpose when I can't seem to find the time to write music, the one thing that I love to do more than ANYTHING in the world?

I play the piano and guitar, but it's composing music for kids that really lifts my spirits. It's the best feeling in the world to write a song for kids and watch them enjoy it. When I'm singing my songs for kids, they clap along, sway back and forth, and even play air-guitar. You should see it, it's quite a sight. It makes me happy, seeing them happy. But is that my life's purpose? I don't know.

Let's be perfectly honest here. The intent of this book is to psyche you up. This book is meant to lift your spirits and encourage you to make a positive difference in your school and community. I have traveled around the country since 1998 speaking to elementary, middle and high school groups. I have been in some top-notch schools and have met wonderful students, talented teachers and compassionate principals. I have seen the best of what your generation has to offer.

However, I have also met a fair share of jerks. Oh, you know the type. They're the ones who send the frazzled substitute teacher to the asylum. The ones who hang out after school to harass a kid half their size. The ones who get completely blitzed and spray paint *Rocko loves Mindy* on national monuments.

Kids aren't the only jerks, of course. There are plenty of adult jerks, too. They're the ones parking their Hummers in the handicapped parking space while they dash in for their non-fat, double-caff grande lattes. The ones who are rude to the waitress and leave no tip. The ones who cut in front of you with a cartload of groceries at the supermarket check-out, when you're merely buying a pack of gum.

Let's face it. Sometimes it can be tough living in this world with jerks, especially if you're a nice guy. And, for better or worse, I'm a nice guy. In fact, I just may be the nicest guy you will every meet. Ask anyone who knows me and they'll tell you the same thing: "That Mark is one nice guy." I remember birthdays, care about other people's feelings, and cry at Hallmark commercials. *Commercials?!* Trust me, when you're hanging out with the guys and you get choked up because little Timmy got a puppy for Christmas, you will get made fun of.

My sensitivity made me an easy target. Here I was, this skinny kid sitting as close to the front row of the bus as possible, picking spitballs out of my hair. At a freshman mixer, some guy came out of nowhere and said, "Hey, why don't you watch where you're going?" and clocked me in the eye. I apologized and backed away, but he hit me again. I ran to a pay phone to call my mom.

As I waited for my mom to pick me up, I thought, *"I apologized to the guy who hit me?"* Clearly this nice guy business wasn't working out.

So I decided to become a jerk. Or at least try.

I became abrupt with telephone solicitors, and impatient with slow cashiers. I watched E.T. with my buddies and *didn't shed a tear!* Oh yeah, I was a tough guy. I was even surly to my own family! Each morning at breakfast I would read the cereal box and ignore them. It was just a matter of time until I pulled my Hummer into the handicapped parking spot to buy my non-fat, double-caff grande latte.

But one day when I saw a lady park her car in the red zone of a supermarket parking lot, I realized there was more to being a jerk than I realized. It was a hot, summer afternoon and she left her keys in the ignition, with her music and air-conditioning blasting, and went inside to shop. She wasn't just running in to pick up some lottery tickets, she was doing some serious shopping! I thought, "How wasteful! How environmentally unsound! How *wrong!*" Filled with self-righteous thoughts, I swaggered over to her car. I considered moving it to the other side of the lot. *That would teach her a lesson!* I considered locking her car doors so when she returned she wouldn't be able to get in. *Ker-pow!* I felt like some sort of moralistic superhero. *"It's a bird, it's a plane, it's Morality Man!"*

I opened her door, turned the engine off, and tossed her keys onto the passenger seat.

A weird thing happened when I drove away. I felt crummy. I could have been arrested! Or even worse, she could have beaten the living snot out of me! Who am I to tell someone how to live her life? Just because I thought someone was being a jerk didn't give me the right to be one. I didn't like how it felt to think like a jerk. I realized I felt better about myself when I have kind thoughts. I *like* how I feel when I make a little kid laugh, or when I'm helping my grandma in and out of her car. I *like* seeing my wife's reaction when I give her a love note. I can't help it. I like being kind. I guess it's just who I am.

We all have a nice guy and jerk inside us. It's our choice which one we want to be.

Check out the choices made by these three high school kids. As a freshman in high school, Mory was encouraged by her parents to make a difference in her world via community service. She focused on homeless children and teenagers in her home city of Chicago. She began by making a few bag dinners each week during the summer and the dinners were distributed at night to the homeless teens. Four years later, Mory, with help from her friends and classmates, stuffed thousands of Christmas stockings with toys, held "bag dinner" parties in the summer, and brightened the lives of thousands of homeless children and teens. Her initial act of kindness snowballed into a movement of love.

Mattie is a best-selling author, past guest on Oprah and a spokesperson for Children's Hospice International on behalf of sick children and their families. Mattie accomplished all of this by the age of twelve, and he did it while restricted to a wheelchair and oxygen tanks. Mattie has a rare form of muscular dystrophy that has already claimed the lives of his three older siblings. Despite his own plight, his poetry is inspirational and life-affirming, and celebrates the miracle of everyday life.

Nickole, a 16-year-old from the state of Washington, created a web site that helps young people share their feelings about violence. Her site (www.y2kyouth.org as of the printing of this book) addresses issues of concern for young people from race to religion to global affairs. She started a violence prevention group, helps teachers create safe schools programming, and averages two hundred hours of volunteering per year.

If kindness is a selfish act, then I think you'll agree that Mory, Mattie and Nickole are very selfish kids. And there are thousands of people grateful for their selfishness.

I believe you feel good when you do good, and that's why I started the Jimmy Project. I met Jimmy in the months following September 11th. Remember that awful day? You could feel the world shift. For months I was glued to the television, consumed by grief. Even asleep I couldn't escape it; my dreams kept replaying those horrific moments. I questioned the purpose of life on earth. How could God allow this to happen?

During this time of struggle, my best friend received some good news. She was pregnant. Yes, my best friend is a girl, not a guy. Of course, a guy helped with the process but it's the girl that gets pregnant. You understand how that works, right? I don't need to draw a diagram, do I? She was going to have a baby. Wow. That made me happy. She didn't have a name picked out yet, so I referred to the unborn child as Jimmy. I wondered what sort of world Jimmy would enter?

Would he/she find hatred or kindness? Discrimination or tolerance? Fear or love?

The answer was up to me.

The Jimmy Project is about spreading kindness wherever you go with the hope that it will come back to all the little Jimmys out there and brighten their world. It's about being kind for no other reason than being kind. And all over the country, young people are performing their own Jimmy Projects every day. It's about deriving selfish pleasure from your acts of kindness. It's a selfish act to give. So be selfish! I encourage you to be selfish…for yourself and for little Jimmy.

Well, you're almost at the end of this chapter. Have you figured out your life's purpose yet? Probably not. I know I haven't. It's not like you can look it up on the Internet. Hey, maybe you can. I'm logging online right now and going to the Ask Jeeves web site. Maybe he knows. Okay, I'm typing in my question: "Jeeves, what is my life's purpose?" Hmm. I've just been led to some inane site with pictures of dancing bunnies and butterflies. I don't think Jeeves has the answer for me.

I guess it takes a lifetime to figure out the big questions. In the meantime, just be kind. You'll be amazed how the rest just falls into place.

When it comes down to it, we all want to be happy *and* we all want to matter. Each of us wants to feel that because we were born, because we walk this earth, somehow, some way we are making a difference. Perhaps, with Jimmy in mind, I can start to make a long-lasting impact on my world and the people in my life.

The Challenge

I challenge *you* to help *me* change the world…for Jimmy. I challenge you to execute three kind things in the next month. I challenge you to perform an act of kindness for a friend, a teacher, and a family member. And make these acts of kindness unique, fun, and creative. Don't just buy your mom flowers - plant her a tree. Don't just leave a sweet note for a teacher - hang a banner of praise. Find out when your friend will be gone, sneak over to his/her house (with parental permission, of course) and clean his/her car. Wouldn't you love to return home to find your car cleaned?

Once you perform these three kind acts, send me an e-mail and tell me about it. My address is mark@markbernstein.com. Brag about yourself, share with me the joy you spread in this world, tell me about your selfishness. Who knows? During these acts of kindheartedness, you may even take a step closer to finding purpose in your everyday life.

Maybe I took one step closer to finding my life's purpose when my friend told me she was pregnant. This friend happens to be my wife. Yup. I'm going to be a father. When little Jimmy is born, he/she is going to look to me to help form his/her opinion of the world. And I'm not taking that for granted. I'm going to do the best I can to fill each moment of Jimmy's life with kindness, tolerance and love.

And I'm going to write some darn good lullabies.

ABOUT THE AUTHOR

Mark Bernstein

Mark began his career as host of his own children's television show on FOX-TV. Currently, he tours the country entertaining and inspiring audiences by relaying his unique perspective on life. Mark challenges his audience with one simple question: what is our purpose on Earth? The answer is...who freakin' knows? Mark has spent his life seeking that answer and is taking steps to find his purpose. Mark is a musician, author, husband, friend, and big fan of "Jimmy." Mark continues to encourage young people to incorporate the principles of "The Jimmy Project" into school and community, and in return, find purpose.

Mark Bernstein Speaks

P.O. Box 30631

Indianapolis, IN 46230

Office: 317-259-4063 Fax: 317-259-4063

Toll Free: 888-572-MARK

Email: mark@markbernstein.com

Web Site: www.markbernstein.com

MIKE PATRICK

Small Deeds and a Few Words Can Be Huge!

CHAPTER

6

Small Deeds and a Few Words Can Be Huge!

Mike Patrick

In 1971, I was a junior in high school with a plan for my life. I knew where I was going. I was a good student with sports on the brain all the time. I played football in the fall, played basketball in the winter, ran track in the spring and played baseball all summer. I was my class vice-president and a member of the student council. School was easy for me. I was passionate about sports. My goal was to get a basketball scholarship for college. I had lots of friends and got along with everyone. The Viet Nam War was raging, but it was on the other side of the world and I really didn't think about it. My world pretty much revolved around my life in a small town in Southwestern Minnesota and whatever sport was in season. I had just gotten my driver's license that spring and was beginning to experience life with the freedom that comes from using the family car once in a while.

On September third, in my first varsity football game, on the second play, everything changed! I wasn't very big, only

5 feet 9 inches tall and weighed 155 pounds. I came into the game in the middle of the second quarter to play free safety; and two plays later, found myself on my back in the end zone, paralyzed, with a 205-pound, all-state fullback lying on top of me. My neck had been broken and my spinal cord damaged when I tried to tackle him. In that instant, I became a quadriplegic. I was paralyzed from the middle of my chest down. I couldn't move my arms or legs; a tingling sensation came over my whole body and the pain in my head was unbearable. I was scared and was trying to figure out what had just happened.

They took me to a hospital that night, and I spent the next seven and one-half months in three different hospitals. I was learning to adjust to my new life in either a power wheelchair or a hospital bed. Five years later, I started telling my story to nursing students at a nursing school close to my home and I have been speaking in schools ever since. I never could have imagined my life would take the sudden turn it did when I came into the game that night.

About fifteen years later, roughly two months after I had spoken at a high school, I was with a friend watching his two sons play a little league baseball game. After the game, we went to Dairy Queen for ice cream and the girl behind the counter handed me a note on the back of a receipt which read: "I am getting help. It's working too. Thanks, I think you saved my life." And then she signed it. I looked up at her and she was smiling from ear to ear. I asked her what she meant. She told me she didn't have time to explain it but she got something from my program. Although I'll never know what it was. I have often wondered what it was I said that had that kind of effect on her. I have her note in my office where I can see it every day.

You never know how your words and actions are going to affect other people. In the summer of 2000, I was flying to Southern California to speak at a teen leadership program. Because my spinal cord injury means I can't walk, I usually fly with my personal care attendant. That trip I flew alone because my younger brother, who lives in California, was going to help me while I was there. I am always the first one on the plane and the last one off. If there is an empty seat in first class, the airlines often put me in the front row just because it is easier to put me there. That particular flight made me look at a lot of things in a very different light.

When the rest of the first class passengers started to board, I recognized the second man. He was an identical twin, who had been a year behind me in high school. He and his brother were minister's kids, good students, who were never in trouble. I looked at him, and at first I wasn't sure which twin he was. All of a sudden, something came over me and I just blurted out, "Percy Kallevig, how are you?"

Remember, it had been about 28 years since I had last seen him. He replied, "Mike, I didn't recognize you. I watched them helping you get on the plane and I wondered to myself – I wonder what Mike Patrick is doing today."

I said with a smile, "Getting on a plane." Since everybody was boarding now, he got in his seat across the aisle and back one row from me. The man standing right behind Percy sat down next to me and I told him one of those "small world" stories about how Percy was a year behind me in school thirty years ago! When everybody else had boarded the plane, Percy leaned forward to try and tell me something. As he did, the man sitting next to me asked if we would like to sit together. They switched places and the next 3 1/2 hours literally changed my life. Percy and I swapped stories reminiscing about the time around my accident.

I remember one story he told which I've used in speeches since then. As I said, Percy's father was a minister and they all went to church on Wednesday nights. Percy asked me if "I remembered a guy by the name of Rick Van Roekel."

"Sure," I said, "he was one of my best friends. He was also our right defensive end on the play when I broke my neck. He is now a head football coach in a high school in Minnesota."

Percy continued, "After church he and I would often go driving around and a couple of times we came out and picked you up and the three of us drove around for a while. I never felt like it was Mike and Rick riding around with Percy, or Mike and Percy riding around with Rick, I always felt like it was Rick and Percy that got to ride around with Mike Patrick."

"Why would you say that? Why did you feel that way?" I asked.

"You were just always one of those special people."

Percy used this really cool analogy about the people on the plane. "There are all those people back in coach class who think we must be something special because we are sitting in first class. We both know why we are really here. You are up here because they couldn't fit you into your seat, so they put you in the front row of first class because it was easy to get you in that seat. I am sitting up here not because the church where I now minister paid for a first class ticket, but because I knew the pilot and they had an empty seat. I got a free flight.

In high school, you were always in first class and we were always just coach. So when you got hurt it affected us all very deeply. I remember where I was the night of your accident. I was at my girlfriend's house and some kids came over after the game. They were all upset and they said Mike Patrick is paralyzed. I'll never forget it, my girlfriend started crying."

I asked him, "Why would she cry? She didn't know me?"

Percy quickly responded, "Everybody knew you. You were friends with everybody. You talked to everybody. I wasn't on the football team, but you still made me feel good about myself. I always knew one day I would get to tell you some of these stories, and now, 29 years after your accident, I am finally getting the chance."

"I didn't think those nights we went driving around were any big deal." I said. That's when I realized they *were* a big deal to Percy.

You never know how the things you say and do are going to affect people. Your words and your actions might make a huge difference to your friends or to that kid you never felt was a part of your group. Don't wait 30 years to tell someone how he or she has affected your life – perhaps only by doing something as simple as riding around in a car or playing on the same team. It might be something you say in the cafeteria, in a classroom or walking home from school. Leaders make a difference every day whether or not they even think about it.

After that conversation, I told Percy part of our conversation would be part of a speech. Percy, who is now a minister, (as is his twin brother) told me, "Oh Mike, some of this is going to be part of a sermon." I've told this story a number of times since then in schools and conferences around the country. That 3 1/2 hour plane trip really made me realize how important the things I say and do really are. I always knew that, but my conversation with Percy made me think about it even more.

I never know what any particular student will take away from one of my speeches. One day a high school student asked me if I could go back and play football again, would I?

I asked, "Do I know I am going to get hurt?"

"Yes."

"No, I would go out for cross country." Pretty much everybody in the gymnasium laughed but him.

"Well, I'm glad you can't go back," he said.

That really shocked me. I asked him, "Why would you say that?"

His response was, "If you went back and didn't play football you wouldn't have gotten hurt and you wouldn't be here with us today."

His comment really hit me! "Maybe I would, but things would just be different. Maybe I would be one of your teachers or one of your coaches."

I have thought about him often and would like to talk to him. I have questions I would like to ask him. I wonder if he remembers that experience? I wonder what possessed him to ask that question?

I often feel like that after I speak. I receive lots of e-mails now and keep in touch with some young people who have stories to tell. They often ask for advice. Sometimes I feel like "Uncle Mike" with kids I don't even know.

I often give someone an ATTITUDE pin at the end of a speech to remind my audience that attitude is a small thing that can make a big difference. I tell them I have something to give them, but the catch is they have to wear it everyday for the rest of their lives. They get this look that says they are not quite sure if they can make that commitment or not. Then I tell them they can trust me. A couple of years ago, I was getting ready to speak to a group of sophomores at a youth health conference when a boy in the front row asked if I remembered him from the fourth grade when I gave him an ATTITUDE pin. My response was that he looked different than he did in the fourth grade and quite honestly I didn't remember him specifically because I had spoken to the fourth graders at that school several years in a row. I gave him a quick once over, looking for his ATTITUDE pin. He wasn't wearing it. I asked him where it was and he quickly replied, "It's on my letter jacket hanging out in the hall." Wow, that was cool!

The thing that was so great about that was he had kept it for six years – and I'm guessing he still has it today. If he thought enough about that pin to put it on his letter jacket and to tell me about it, my presentation must have really affected him that day in the fourth grade. What can you do for a fourth grader to make a difference that could affect them for the rest of their life? What can somebody else say and do to you that would have a positive impact on your life? You are a member of a group or a team that has an opportunity to impact your school and possibility your whole community. How does your attitude affect the people in your life?

If I asked you to make a list of all of your negative attributes and all of your positive attributes, which list would be longer? What does that tell you about yourself? How do your negative and positive attributes affect your team, your group, your class, your school and your community?

I have found my reason for being. I know why I broke my neck. I hope some day you find your reason for being and understand why you have the attitudes you do. Your behavior has far reaching consequences you may never realize. Your attitude determines what sort of effect you have on people you may never remember meeting or interacting with.

I CHALLENGE YOU!

Do you remember when you were a little kid of seven or eight years old and there was a high school boy or girl that lived on your block or across the street who used to play catch with you, or spend time with you, and you couldn't wait to grow up so you could be like him or her? What sort of effect do you have on your younger siblings or little kids that live down the street from you?

The next time you cross paths with a little kid in your neighborhood or in a mall, go out of your way to make it a positive experience for them. Give them a positive experience they will never forget. Take the time to make a difference in the life of a child.

It's said that everybody has a story. The little kid down the street from you will someday grow up and they, too, will have a story to tell. Make it your mission to have impacted them in such a positive way they will not be able to tell their story without mentioning your name.

ABOUT THE AUTHOR

Mike Patrick

Mike got the electric chair and lived to tell about it – the electric wheelchair, that is. Mike is a motivational speaker and health educator with good news to tell. The good news is, we are all very capable people. We all need to recognize those capabilities and then learn to use them. Mike helps you do just that with candor, wit and humor. What he has to say will make you laugh. Some of it will make you cry. He will guarantee you this, it will make you "Think About It."

Patrick Communications, Inc.
3225 Emerson Avenue South
Minneapolis, MN 55408-3523
612-827-4110 Fax: 612-824-9229
Toll Free: 800-972-9537
E-mail: mike@patcom.com
Web Site: www.patcom.com

BYRON V. GARRETT

Live Your Life on Purpose

CHAPTER

7

Live Your Life on Purpose

Byron V. Garrett

Throughout my travels, I've had the opportunity to meet people who cross all spectrums of society. I've met those who have gone from luxury avenue to losing lane and from losing lane to luxury avenue. The biggest secret to making a difference rests within living your life on purpose.

It's Your Thing – Do What You Wanna Do!

While growing up as a teen a popular song gained national recognition which is still very real today, "it's your thing, do what you wanna do!" It is very difficult to make a difference when you are not living your life on purpose. As we journey through life, we are faced with many difficult decisions and tough choices for which we will later be held accountable.

While you are growing up you <u>must</u> realize the power of the choices that you make now. Did you know that what you decide today has a direct impact on the rest of your life? Most people don't get it, they really miss the boat.

Everything you do now has a direct impact on what you can and cannot do later.

I know many people simply dislike school. There are dozens of reasons why people dislike school including the teacher, other students, the lunch, as well as too much or not enough homework. In most cases we dislike school because it is a "have to" situation. We have people tell us when we can eat, who we sit next to, what classes we should take, where we can and cannot go – school is full of directions and instructions. I considered it to be almost like the military because we are even told when we can go do number 1 or number 2. Our reasons for disliking school are actually irrelevant.

Even though school is a "have to" situation, it is the critical link to getting us to the point of doing the things we "want to" do. Time and time again we have been presented with the fact that the more education you have, the greater your opportunities for success. During high school you learn information that you don't consider to be important but then again you don't get it.

You should use your education as an opportunity to gain information and insight to determine what you want to do. So many people are frustrated, mad and just plum crazy because they are not doing what they want to do, but rather what they have to do and there is a distinct difference.

I frequent fast food restaurants about 2 times per week. As I visit, I always wonder when I see an adult working at McDonalds or Burger King, if they are working there because they want to or because they have to in order to make ends meet. Don't miss my point, it does not matter where you work be it Microsoft or Taco Bell, American Express or Wal-Mart as long as you are doing it because you want to, not because you have to. People are always quick to say… "I have bills to pay", "I have a child to care for", and a host of other responses. In reality, most people do the things they do because they "have to" instead of because they "want to". There reasoning lies within accepting responsibility for the choices they have made. It's that simple.

If you truly want to make a difference in life, you can begin by figuring out your thing – your purpose and doing it.

Always Deliver

In society today, much time is spent on customer service training and teaching people how to work effectively with each other. Companies have adopted the slogan "customer - #1." With that in mind, it becomes our responsibility to exceed the expectations of those around us. When you look in the mirror each morning, you should be a person of strong character, high integrity and great self-worth. You need to be a "go to" person. A person people look to for direction, one that others can depend on when needed. In short, you have to be a person who always delivers.

Dr. Martin Luther King, Jr. offered great words beyond his infamous "I Have A Dream" speech. He stated, "if it falls your lot to be a street sweeper, then sweep streets like Michelangelo painted pictures, like Shakespeare wrote poetry, like Beethoven composed music…sweep streets so well that all the hosts of heaven and earth would pause and say here lies a great street sweeper who swept his job well."

The words of Dr. King will echo throughout history. The fact is no matter your station, position, rank, or class you have to be a person who is doing his or her job so well that people pause and wonder, how do you do what you do. As a little boy, I learned that the mailman delivers mail under three conditions – rain, sleet or snow. I was always amazed that if a stamp was not on the envelope it would be returned to sender. The delivery of the mail had little to do with the weather conditions, but more to do with the stamps ability to stick to it. I don't know what has happened to you thus far in life, but you must stick to it until you deliver. If you've been abused, neglected, mistreated, whatever your situation – I'm truly sorry. Beyond the apology awaits the fact that you have to make a conscious decision to do something different or your life will never change.

The rain in your life may have been losing your boyfriend or girlfriend to your best friend, I don't know. Perhaps the sleet in your life has been a teacher or someone else from school continually telling you that you're not good enough and don't have what it takes to make it. I don't know. Maybe the snow in your life has been your father or mother walking out and giving up on you, I honestly don't know. But I do know this – in spite of the rain, in spite of sleet, and certainly in spite of the snow you have to be like a stamp and stick to it until you deliver. When you are living your life on purpose, you deliver. No ifs, ands, or buts about it. You always deliver.

No One Can Beat You Being You

Throughout life you will quickly discover that it does not pay to be anyone other than yourself. Many people have spent their lives and thousands of dollars trying to be like someone else. In school students try to emulate, replicate, duplicate and imitate the lives of others around them and people they see on television.

I'm certain everyone has wanted or admired the life of someone else at some point in time or another. In understanding the concept of living your life on purpose you must remember the most critical element – LIVE YOUR LIFE! There is nothing worse than trying to be a success by living the life of someone else. You have a specific design and calling upon your life. The sooner you begin to identify and fulfill your purpose in life, the greater your opportunity for success.

The poet Douglas Mallock stated, "if you can't be a pine on top of the hill, be a shrub in the valley; be the best little shrub by the side of the hill, if you can't be a bush – be a tree. If you can't be a highway, be a trail – if you can't be the sun, be a star. For it isn't by size that you win or fall just be the best of whatever you are."

Being the best does not involve competition with anyone. Remember, there is only one human race. We spend so much time trying to outdo each other. Imagine what life would be like if we focused on lifting others rather than tearing others down. Competition usually results from two or more people trying to do the same thing. If you are focused on your walking worthy of your purpose you will find peace, joy and happiness. Don't get me wrong, there will always be haters. No way around that; however, you can rest assured that you are making a difference by fulfilling your purpose. I have discovered that there are days when others will not offer guidance or encouragement, but rather you must encourage yourself. If no one else believes in you, you must believe in yourself.

So what exactly does it mean that no one can beat you being you? Once you have discovered your purpose or calling in life and are striving in that direction no one can beat you being you. The reality is that each person must focus on that which they are to accomplish; nothing more, nothing less. I believe Chris Rock is an outstanding comedian and talented actor. While interviewing Chris some time ago for a film, I discovered that he goes through a lengthy process of having people assist him. Someone does his hair and makeup, someone else selects his clothing while yet another person provides insight regarding the reading of the script. When shooting the film Chris may have as many as 5 people tending to his every need to assist him in being "Chris Rock."

I firmly believe that any individual that has a team of people whose sole responsibility is to help them be the best person they can be at that moment is destined for greatness. I can only imagine if I had such a team how awesome I would be. Yet, I'm a realist. I don't have a team of 5 or even 1 for that matter. It's just me working on becoming the best me I can be. No one to do my clothing, no person charged with styling my hair and no one to help me study my lines. The old proverb rings true, "if it's going to be, it's up to me."

It's a Matter of Choice

Time waits for no man or woman. Being a man or woman is a matter of birth but being a man or woman who makes a difference is a matter of choice. You have to choose to be uncommon. Choose to be dependable and reliable. Choose to exceed expectations. It is your right to choose the life you want to live.

Many people are confused. They believe that their present condition determines their future. Your future has yet to be created so everything you do until it arrives will shape, create and bring into existence what it will be. It makes no difference whether you live in a 5 bedroom house, a 2 bedroom apartment or 1 room shack. It makes no difference if your father is a janitor or if your mother is a CEO. It makes no difference if you ride in an Excursion, Expedition, Explorer, Escape or Escort. Your entire future is a matter of choice.

Whether you live a life of peace, joy and happiness or one of misery and discomfort is completely up to you. Many people spend their entire life blaming other folks. When I was a little boy I learned that every time you point one finger at someone you have four others pointing back at you. You have to make a conscious decision to do something different if you want your life to change. The world owes you nothing. Let's just keep it real. Everyone needs or wants an apology for something, but only a few choose to accept responsibility for where they are and make the decision to press forward.

Eleanor Roosevelt said, "no person can make you feel inferior without your consent." In other words, if you feel bad about your present situation it's due to the fact of how you allow people to make you feel. Again, you choose to let someone's opinion of you become who you are. I choose not to live down or up to anyone's expectations of me. Now don't get me wrong, I realize that I am on this planet with billions of other people; however, I am not going to give you so much clout and credence over my life that I jump when you say jump or I crawl when you say crawl. No person should have that much power over you unless you allow them. I refuse to give away my freedom.

If you think about it even as babies we choose when to crawl, when to walk, and when to talk. For those of you thinking on a scientific plane, follow my thought process for a moment before you get side tracked. As a student you choose to go to school and/or pay attention. You choose to do homework, even if you don't understand it, you choose to attempt it or not. Life is full of people who believe they lack the power to choose. I want you to know that you have that power and it is awesome when used correctly.

Life is full of choices. My hope, my wish, my prayer is that you make solid, healthy choices with an eye towards the future. In society we are always faced with options to choose and decisions to make at the moment; however, you should already know what happens when you choose to have five minutes of fun and forget about tomorrow. I've seen young people around the globe throw away sport championships and academic scholarships for making poor choices the night before a big game or a scholarship interview. I was watching the show American Idol and the contestants were asked to work in groups and prepare a routine for the following day. Note, these individuals had competed and won a trip to Hollywood in hopes of being a finalist and receiving a lucrative recording contract. Each and every performance is critical. However, on this night 3 of the contestants chose to go out and party, staying out late not getting the proper rest needed. It was as if they thought this one evening would not ruin their chance of success. I cannot honestly say that it blew their chance completely but it sure had an impact. My question to you is why risk it in the 1st place?

MAD Is a Continuous State

Powerful people of strong character are those who make the right decision when no one is looking. I challenge you to decide today, not tomorrow to be a person who makes the right choice. I challenge you to find something worth dying for but you live to make it a reality for someone else. I challenge you to look pessimism in the face and say "I don't think so", I'm bigger than this. I challenge you to enroll others to begin living their lives on purpose.

I used to think there was one road map leading to success. Unfortunately, no such map exists. The upside to that is you get to map out your own success on your terms. In your life you will have the opportunity to own and operate, research and write, explore and discover as well as lead or be led. I hope that you choose a life that gives you happiness that money cannot afford. Choose a life that gives a pillow of peace and a cushion of confidence. If you do not choose the life you want to live, the life you live will choose you. Lastly, understand that you have the right to live any kind of life you want. I only hope that you choose to live your life on purpose with a goal of making a difference.

ABOUT THE AUTHOR

Byron V. Garrett

President & CEO of Life Works International, Byron V. Garrett is a highly sought after speaker, leadership consultant and personal coach. Also known as SPKR4LIFE (speaker 4 life), Mr. Garrett has presented in Nigeria, Canada, the Caribbean and most of the United States.

Mr. Garrett was recently appointed as a Special Assistant for School Readiness and Youth Development to the Governor's Office in Arizona. Mr. Garrett is the Co-Founder of Progressive Schools and serves as Pastor of Civic and Community Affairs at Greater Progressive Christian Church. Mr. Garrett is an Educational Doctorate Candidate at Pepperdine University.

Mr. Garrett has authored several books including **The ABC's of Life** and has interviewed Chris Rock, Vanessa Williams, Samuel Jackson, Jude Law and a number of other celebrities.

Byron V. Garrett, President & CEO
Life Works International
9406 W. Hazelwood Street, Phoenix, AZ 85037
Office: 602-763-3041 Fax: 602-523-9091
Email: spkr4life@lifeworks101.com
Web Site: www.byrongarrett.com

PATTY HENDRICKSON

Bother to Be a Role Model

CHAPTER

8

Bother to Be a Role Model

Patty Hendrickson

Jane Goodall is famous for working with chimpanzees throughout the world. Her respect and nurturing affection for animals is incredible. Jane says, *Above all we must realize that each of us makes a difference with our life. Each of us impacts the world around us every single day. We have a choice to use the gift of our life to make the world a better place – or not to bother.* Wow. Yes, indeed we should bother every single day to make a difference with our life – to be a role model. Even though some of us struggle with feeling different and alone, we need to bother to make a difference.

Do you sometimes feel you're out of place – Like you don't really fit in? It's as if the rest of the world is tuned to Channel 3 and you're hearing Channel 4. You don't know what it is, but you feel out of balance. There is something missing.

I understand what you're feeling and you're not alone. There is an epidemic of feeling out of balance or dissatisfied. We want so badly to feel personal peace. This dissatisfaction or stress is internal and it can make you feel sad, tired and very uneasy. It's a general uncomfortableness with who and where you are.

[Quick Time-out Comment. The amazing fact that you can relate to that feeling and you're reading this chapter and this book makes it even more important. I know you aren't just wasting your time reading because you have nothing better to do. You're reading this book for a reason. You want more. You expect more out of yourself. You are one of those people who see the need to make a difference. And even with those feelings of passion you too can relate to the feeling of being out of balance or not fitting in sometimes. Time-in.]

This epidemic of feeling out of balance or dissatisfied comes from the GAP. No, not the store, but the gap in our lives. It's the gap between the actions of our lives – "the doing," and the beliefs of our lives – "the knowing." When "the doing" and "the knowing" don't match, we feel dissatisfied.

Let me explain. Most of us know what we should do – make time for ourselves, exercise, invest in healthy relationships with family and friends, and give our best to school, work and activities. We feel stress or dissatisfaction when our actions don't match our intentions. There is a space between what we know and what we do. The wider the gap between "the knowing" and "the doing," the more dissatisfied we feel.

How do we deal with this feeling of being dissatisfied? It's not easy. It takes hard work, but the payoff is huge. Investing the time to close the gap is how you make a difference. Being a confident person in your choices and beliefs helps you serve as a role model to the world.

Each of us has a core of potential. Our journey in this life is to continue to push, try, expand and experiment with our desires, needs and skills to fulfill this potential. Every time we try something new we are growing into ourselves. As we grow into ourselves and find what feels naturally good to us, we are discovering our own truth. Nelson Mandela said, *Our deepest fear is not that we are inadequate. It is that we are powerful beyond measure.* The more we try new things and discover our own potential, the fuller our lives become. The things we want and enjoy become clearer. But how or where do we start to find this truth?

There isn't a simple answer. But here are a few places to start on your journey of bothering to make a difference and finding your own truth.

1. Focus on Your Good Stuff
2. Understand Yourself and Your Space
3. Take Action

Focus on Your Good Stuff.

The strongest place to operate from is your strengths or where you are most competent. Your competence leads to your confidence. And when you feel confident you are more likely to be successful.

Many years ago I went back to college to get my Masters Degree. It was very time consuming but a very positive opportunity for me. I got my degree, but more important was a very positive learning experience that happened one random night in October. Allow me to share –

We were required to take only two tests in this class – a mid-term and a final. And if you got anything less than a "B" (like a C, D, or F) you would be asked to leave the class and the program. So it was very important to study and do well on the mid-term. I studied like a mad woman and was thoroughly prepared. That night I took the exam, turned it in to my professor and felt really good about my performance.

At the start of the next class my professor returned our tests. I was smiling from ear to ear waiting for my good grade. When I looked down my expression turned from jubilation to utter terror. The whole first page of the exam was a sea of red marks, checks and circles. I looked through the entire exam. Yikes! There were only three places where I didn't have an ugly red mark.

Immediately my abusive mental critic – you know, that voice in your head – started having a field day. *You idiot! Don't cry. What a twit! I can't believe you screwed up so bad. Just sit here, you dork. Don't cry. You blew it! You are getting kicked out of here. LOSER!*

While giving myself a mental beating, I was totally unaware of my professor standing in front of the class, looking at us, and rocking back and forth on his heels. Finally, he said, *Congratulations!*

I thought, *You jerk.*

He said, *You all look a bit perplexed. Allow me to explain. You see I mark what you answer correctly.* I let out the biggest sigh of relief. Whew!

He continued, *You know what you don't do well. I want to draw attention to what you do well.*

That is one of the wisest things I've ever heard. *You know what you don't do well. I want to draw attention to what you do well.* How many of us spend time looking at others and trying to measure up to their skills? How many of us focus on what we don't do well? Instead, we need to look very hard at what we're good at and what we like to do. We need to find those parts of us that make us feel totally alive and vibrant.

We don't know each other personally, so I can't use your particular talents, but I happen to be an athletic person who is short – about 5'2" on a good day. Now, I can work really hard becoming a skilled ball handler and a contributing member on a basketball team. But no matter how hard I practice and perfect my skills, I probably will not excel at rebounding. Yes, I can jump high and aggressively, but I'm short. This is a reality.

When we focus on our good stuff, we focus on those talents and desires that we enjoy. We operate from the space of our competence. Remember, our competence leads to our confidence. To start your journey of discovering your truth, consider what is it that you're good at or really enjoy doing. This is an excellent place to start to close the gap and fill your potential to make a difference as a role model to the world.

Understand Yourself and Your Space.

Here's an obvious dose of reality – You are with yourself all the time. But just because you are with something often, doesn't mean you know it. I'll prove it to you.

Right now, grab a pen and draw two circles at least an inch wide. On one of the circles draw the front side of a penny and draw the back side of a penny on the other circle. Just a reminder – No one will grade you on your drawing and no cheating. Go ahead. I'll wait. **** (I'm humming the Jeopardy theme song.) ****

Now look at a penny. How many parts or elements did you correctly draw? Did you remember the word "Liberty" on the front? Which way is Abe Lincoln's head facing? Did you remember the phrase "E Pluribus Unum?" – which means "Out of the many, one" – on the back side. Whether you actually drew the circles or just tried to picture it in your mind, I bet you weren't able to recall all of the elements.

The US Mint says that we touch about 1,000 pennies every year. Those of us who work retail jobs touch even more. So if we touch something that many times, why don't we know what it looks like? Hmmm. Yes, you're familiar with a penny because it's the only copper colored coin in your pocket and it has flat edges. But just because we are familiar with something doesn't mean we are knowledgeable of it. The same can be said about ourselves. Just because you are with yourself all the time doesn't mean you know yourself.

Neal Walsh said, *If you do not go within, you go without.* He is speaking a simple truth. We need to invest the time to explore ourselves. If we don't explore ourselves we go without the understanding to fulfill our own potential.

So often when we feel the most hurried and stressed is when we need the biggest rest or time to reflect. It is the time away from deadlines and demands that helps clarify what is most important. Plan a total diversion from whatever is happening in your life. Your rest can take many forms – time to simply clean your room (which can be very therapeutic for some); a trip to some remote place where no one can find you; an afternoon curled up with a book; a day of rigorous physical activity (yes, for some this is great rest or down-time from the normal routine). The rest is simply time away from your routine.

The penny has specific elements. What are the specific elements that make you who you are? Be on the lookout for those things you experience that bring you the most joy. Heck, write them down. Take the time to understand yourself and your space.

Take Action – Build Momentum.

Here's a beautiful quote from one of my favorite philosophers – Oprah Winfrey. Oprah says, *My philosophy is that not only are you responsible for your life, but doing the best at this moment puts you in the best place for the next moment.* Now that is definitely an attitude of action to bother to become a role model.

Yes, we need to focus on our good stuff and understand ourselves. You are serving as a role model as you discover your own truth. But we also need to take action with the information we learn about ourselves. The action is what puts us in the best place to serve as a role model. It's so easy to talk about what we know. It's much harder and more rewarding to serve as an example with our actions.

What have you done today to put yourself in a positive place of action? Hmmm. It doesn't have to be something monumental, but it needs to be something. As we start to take action we naturally build momentum. What do I mean by taking action?

Actively choose to do things every day that make you feel alive. Do those things that fulfill you.

- Maybe you enjoy listening to some particular music. Commit to listening to that music some time every day.
- Maybe you enjoy hanging out with a friend who makes you laugh. Commit to regularly sharing time with that friend.
- Maybe you enjoy playing an instrument. Commit to regularly playing that instrument.
- Maybe you feel better when you skateboard. Commit some time every day to skateboarding.
- Maybe you feel better when you workout. Commit to regularly working out.
- Maybe you feel better when you write in your journal. Commit to regularly writing in your journal.
- Maybe you feel better when you make others smile. Commit to making others smile everyday. Heck, make a game of it. Plan to make 30 people smile on Tuesday.
- Maybe you enjoy reading inspirational quotes. (This is one of my favorites.) Commit to looking for inspirational material every day.

It's amazing how much more fulfilled you'll start feeling when you take action and start building momentum. You'll also start to feel more confident. And when that happens, you can start to make huge strides serving as a role model. Here are some things you could do at school right away to make a difference.

- Make a commitment to look one quiet, shy student in the eye and smile at them.
- Commit to anonymously thank a teacher who looks like they need a pat on the back.
- Commit to saying "good job" to at least three people tomorrow.

You may think these things are too small to make a difference, but you're wrong. Every year nearly 5,000 young people take their own lives. Most of these people have had the feelings of being out of balance and not belonging. Your simple action of reaching out and connecting with them – even if it is only a smile – can be a lifeline.

Remember what Jane Goodall said. *Above all we must realize that each of us makes a difference with our life. Each of us impacts the world around us every single day. We have a choice to use the gift of life to make the world a better place – or not to bother.*

I'm so glad you're choosing to bother to be a role model.

ABOUT THE AUTHOR

Patty Hendrickson, CSP

For over 15 years Patty Hendrickson has been sharing her enthusiastic message throughout America and beyond. She is the author of the inspirational book – *Who I Am Depends On Me!* – now in its fourth printing. Patty is a Certified Speaking Professional, a designation earned by less than 500 people in the world. Whether she's speaking to a group of 20 leaders or 2,000 members, Patty's programs are always high-energy and interactive. *Patty's energy inspires, so her message sticks!*

Patty specializes in leadership conferences and officer training. She most often speaks about leadership, teams and motivation.

Hendrickson Leadership Group, Inc.
N. 1601 Lost Ridge Road
La Crosse, WI 54601
Toll Free: 800-557-2889
Email: Patty@PattyHendrickson.com
Web Site: www.pattyhendrickson.com

KEITH HAWKINS

The Game

CHAPTER

9

The Game

Keith Hawkins

A speaker once said, "If 200 people take this positive message out to ten people and those ten people share the message with ten others, and so on, within twenty five days the whole world would know." After hearing that message I knew I would be one of those 200 people. I knew one day I would make a difference, but at that time I didn't understand how.

As a young kid I would have disagreed with this speaker. Growing up I didn't think my existence even mattered. I was another poor kid growing up without a father in the tough Los Angeles area. All I knew and saw was struggle, suffering, and pain. In fact, during this time I had become a negative, bitter, lonely, and confused person. Little did I know my life was about to change, and it would start with a simple game of basketball.

During my freshman year of high school, my friend convinced me to run for sophomore class president. Being a loud mouth kid, my friends thought I should put it to work in student council. When I won, I was forced to go to leadership camp at Santa Barbara University. During camp breaks, my friend Rick and I would play basketball against all challengers. Within two days Rick and I were considered the best "ballers" at camp.

During one break we were playing ball and I noticed an older guy watching us play. I asked Rick who he was. Rick said, "Oh that's Phil Boyte, he's a motivational speaker." At first I thought he wanted to play, but then I looked at him closely, and he didn't look like a ball player. His shorts were too short, he hunched over, and his shoes looked like a throw back from the old Boston Celtics. I was thinking this guy couldn't play ball with us.

Then Phil walked over and yelled, "I'll play you." I couldn't help from laughing. He said, "If you think you're that good, why don't you play me and my friend Norm?"

We told them we didn't play for free and asked them what they wanted to play for. Phil replied, "We'll play for your hats."

"Fine." I said, "When we win what will you guys give us?"

"Does it matter? You're going to win anyway, right?" Phil answered.

We decided to make the show down at lunch. Lunch time came quickly and sure enough half the camp was there to watch. Rick and I walked on the court early to get some practice. Phil and Norm were no where to be found. They showed up twenty minutes later smiling ear to ear. I could tell they didn't have a clue how badly they were about to get embarrassed.

I looked at Phil and said, "What's up?"

Phil grinned and replied, "The sky."

I laughed it off. "Why are you guys just getting here?"

Norm said they wanted to eat before they beat us. I couldn't believe it, these guys are weak and they ate before the game. I actually started to feel sorry for them!

Before we started Phil asked, "So where can I pick up my hat?"

I couldn't believe what I was hearing, this guy really thought he had a chance to win. It was game time.

Rick and I huddled up to discuss our strategy. "OK Rick, you take the white guy, he looks pretty weak. I'll take the black guy, he might have some skills."

We let the old guys take the ball out first. Phil passed the ball to Norm and he could hardly dribble. It was going to be easier than I thought. The black guy couldn't play either. After Norm almost tripped over the ball, he passed it to Phil. Phil shot the ball immediately. I looked up and I couldn't believe it. The ball went in.

Grinning from ear to ear, Phil gave me the ball, "Loser take's out."

"Nah, nah, where we come from winners take out." Phil smiled and took the ball out.

Every time Norm got the ball he quickly passed it to Phil. Two more shots went up, swish after swish. The whole crowd was cheering and it wasn't for us. Rick and I finally got the ball. It is was our time to shine. I gave the ball to Rick who shot his signature scoop shot, and it went in. Of course, after our first shot we started to brag.

Rick passed the ball to me, I shot it right over Norm…swish. I passed it to Rick. He started out with his Magic hook shot but he bricked it. Phil got the ball from long range, he threw up what I thought was a prayer. Swish! Rick walked over to me gasping for air. I asked Rick what was wrong. I will never forget the crazy look Rick gave me.

Rick said, "Keith, the white guy you thought wasn't good is running circles around me, while the black guy you thought had "skills," hasn't scored a single basket. That's what's wrong with me."

"OK, fine. I'll guard Phil, you take Norm." I looked Phil dead in his eyes. "Now lets see if you can score on me." I fired back with my cocky attitude.

Phil is right handed so I forced him left. He went up for a shot. I couldn't believe my eyes. He shot it left handed, swish! I couldn't believe this guy was actually good. The score was eleven to seven, we were losing.

Phil passed it to Norm. Norm rushed the basket and threw the ball over his head. Somehow the ball grew knees and the shot crawled in. The crowd went wild. Everyone rushed the court and started to give Phil and Norm high fives. Rick and I walked off trying not to be noticed, but everyone started to give us a hard time.

I learned one thing from Phil during that game. White men might not be able to jump but they sure can shoot. Afterward, Rick and I walked over to Phil and Norm to give them our hats. Phil laughed and said, "Thanks, but no thanks. We just wanted to teach you a lesson." Little did I know this wouldn't be the last lesson Phil would teach me. In fact the lesson was just beginning.

The next day I saw that Phil Boyte was going to be our keynote speaker, so I got our student council to go watch him.

Phil was introduced and told an incredible story I will never forget. It was about a kid who played basketball after school by himself at the park. One particular day he noticed balloons flying over his head. The kid was intrigued by the balloons and walked over to sec where they were coming from. As he walked through the park he noticed the man with the balloons. As the kid approached the cart, the man looked at the kid and said "Hi" but the kid didn't reply. The man noticed this kid was different. The kid had a deformed arm. Starring at the man, the kid said, "Sir, I notice the balloons in the air are all one color and perfectly round. Is this the only way a balloon will float...does it have to be perfect?" The man paused not knowing what to say. He could see right away this kid was treated differently because of his arm. The man finally replied, "A balloon doesn't have to be a certain color. It could be black, orange, white, yellow, red, blue, it doesn't matter, it will still fly. The shape can be round, long, short, skinny, fat, it wouldn't matter, it will still fly. Kid, it's not the outside appearance that makes us who we are, it's the stuff on the inside." The man tied a balloon to the kid, and he ran back to play basketball.

When Phil finished his story he looked right at me and said, "Keith it doesn't matter what color you are or what you look like. It's not the stuff on the outside that makes you who you are, it is the stuff on the inside."

All the students looked at me when Phil said my name. My eyes filled with tears. I remember feeling a huge empty hole in my heart. All I wanted was for someone to care for me and love me. Up to that point I felt so empty. I treated people with the same emptiness. I never had a father figure in my life. I didn't think anyone cared, but Phil showed me something different. "People don't care how much you know until you show them how much you care," Phil said at the end of his speech.

Phil had opened my eyes, mind, and heart. My stereotypical views of people became a part of who I was. The sad part was, people were following me because I was thought of as a leader.

After his speech, Phil talked to me about taking action. "Keith, you have a gift, but if you don't share your gift you will lose it."

"What are you talking about? You don't even know me," I replied.

I will never forget what he said, "Faces change but attitudes stay the same. Keith, challenge your attitude. Don't worry about the way you or anybody else looks. Take action."

He walked away leaving me to think about what taking action really meant. I wanted to be a better person and now I had someone who cared and knew I could be better. I couldn't let Phil down. I was now focused, recharged, and fired up. I was going to create something bigger than me. I was about to make a difference in other people's lives, just like Phil did in mine.

As we headed back on the bus to Garey High School, my friend, Teddy, looked pretty sad and I asked him what was wrong. He said, "Man, I wish our school could be like camp. At camp everyone really cared about each other."

After hearing Teddy's answer I knew something had to change. I also knew changing others would be impossible if I didn't change first. So, I decided I would change and then I would get my team behind me. I was compelled from that moment to stand and speak from the bottom of my heart. "Why couldn't our school be like camp? Camp doesn't seem like the real world, but it was real and they gave us the tools to make our school real too. We must take action, if we don't who will?"

Afterwords, my advisor, Mr. Rizzi stood up and addressed the whole student council. "Keith is right, it starts with action, and the action must come from you." Mr. Rizzi turned to me and said, "Phil would be proud of you, I know I am." I thanked him and thought with school starting in two weeks, my biggest challenge was ahead of me.

I kept reminding myself to take action. I thought the best way I could do that was to get involved in every club, sport, and social group I could. With all this involvement my grades started to drop. People in student council started to talk behind my back.

Mr. Rizzi even had a meeting with me about my situation. I asked him to give me a second chance, and I was thankful that he did. He told me that Phil Boyte was coming to speak to our school. I couldn't believe it, the coolest guy I had ever met was coming to our school!

When Phil saw me that day, he gave me a hug. I couldn't believe it. I had never been hugged by a guy. I had to tell him, "Phil, at my school guys don't hug, we shake…OK?" But truthfully, his hug made me feel like he considered me a friend.

When he spoke to the student body, everyone in the gym was silent and was thoroughly involved in Phil's message. Later that day, Phil came to the student council meeting to speak to us. He was talking about being accountable for our actions. I was sitting up front making snide comments after everything Phil said.

Phil looked at me and I knew he had heard enough. "Why are you talking?" Phil asked. "The number one person who needs to be more responsible for their actions is you. What kind of message do you send to your peers as a leader when your actions are as poor as theirs? You better get it together because this student council needs you."

Phil was real with me, and my respect for him sky-rocketed. Never before had a speaker at our school spent time getting to know us. All I had heard from speakers before was "Be positive, and you will stay motivated." But Phil told us, "Motivation doesn't come from a speaker, motivation comes from effort, and effort comes from you." Phil taught us that if you are real, others will follow you because you give them a sense of trust. As a leader you must take action, and through your actions you must be real. And when you are real, people will trust you.

Our biggest obstacle as a student council was the fact that we weren't *real.* There were those in our student council who were there just to put an impressive credential on their college application. Others joined for the activities. And some were there just because they were popular. The other students on campus saw right through this. Many student council members had simply forgotten what student council was all about. They forgot that activities don't make the school; people do. We needed to stop worrying about activities and start taking care of people.

The next year I became junior class president. Administrators, teachers, and students expected the best out of me. Leading by example and creating an alliance of people who cared, I saw the culture of my school change. Upper classmen stopped beating up the freshman. Students began showing more respect for teachers. There was noticeably less graffiti on the walls, and more people started getting involved in student activities.

I attributed this change to being a walking example on my campus. One of my favorite quotes was, "People don't listen to what you say, they look at what you do." Each day I reminded my student council how important this was if we were going to make a difference. My school was becoming a better place for everyone and I felt I was becoming a better leader.

My senior year I became the ASB president. I couldn't believe that in four short years I went from a lonely freshman to being one of the most influential students on campus. I spoke to Phil about this responsibility.

Phil advised me, "Keith all you have to do is believe in yourself and believe in the people around you. Always keep expectations high for yourself and for those who you lead."

I had high expectations for everyone and every group on campus. I expected all the students to be involved with activities. I expected upper classmen to be role models, and I expected student council members to be the best leaders they could be. Our school climate became happier and our culture was one where students and teachers genuinely cared for each other.

Late in the spring we had a final pep rally, and it was the best ever! Afterwards I had the student council reflect back to the bus ride from camp three years ago. We wanted our school to be like leadership camp; a place where people were happy. Our journey to make this happen was tough, but we did it. We all knew that we had steered the school back to the right path. We were all very proud.

I reminded the ASB members that, "Student council used to be about activities, now it's about people." I felt that we had accomplished our mission. We had truly made a difference. That meeting was a happy time for everyone, especially me. I had gone from being a selfish, empty person who didn't care, to a person who wanted to make a difference in students' lives.

I owed a debt of gratitude to Phil Boyte. He made a difference in my life. He inspired me to become a speaker and help students the same way he helped me.

I moved to Chico, California and stayed with Phil and his family. Phil mentored me in the ways of speaking, but more importantly in the ways of life. Phil and his family have become an important part of my life. In fact, ten years later Phil was the best man in my wedding, and he is still one of my best friends today.

Sometimes I think about how this all started with a basketball game. It evolved into a friendship where Phil taught me three important leadership skills. First, accept others who are different, and see past the outside. Second, be real. When you are, people will trust and believe in you. Third, believe in yourself. Be the absolute best you can be and people around you will become better. Combining these skills will give you the necessary steps to take action. Go back to your school and lead people through your actions. Phil shared this challenge with me now I share it with you.

The more confidence you have in yourself the more the people you lead have in themselves. If you successfully follow through with these three steps there is no doubt you will create a positive change at home, in school, and your community. You can make a difference through the power of taking action.

ABOUT THE AUTHOR

Keith Hawkins

Keith Hawkins is a national youth speaker who travels the United States and Canada speaking to over 200,000 students each year. Keith has spoken at the United Nations, is featured in a national communication text entitled Between One and Many, and co-authored Teen Power and Beyond. Keith's desire to influence students is felt by all who hear him. Keith is inspired by his wife and best friend Lori. They're vision is to create an environment that supports today's youth empowering them to fulfill their dreams.

Keith dedicates his chapter to Phil Boyte and his family for all their support and love. You have truly made a difference in my life. The gift you have given me continues to make a difference by inspiring the lives of our youth. You will always be my family.

Thank You.

Keith Hawkins
1308 Crystal Hollow Ct., Lincoln, CA 95648
916-408-7129 Fax: 916-408-7128
Toll Free: 888-604-4295 (HAWK)
Email:hawksmx@aol.com
Web Site: www.keithhawkins.com

RYAN UNDERWOOD

Rise to the Top

How to Exude Class and Leave an Impression that Lasts!

CHAPTER

10

Rise to the Top

How to Exude Class and Leave an Impression that Lasts!

Ryan Underwood

You're hired! You're fired.
Right on! Right on your way.
You're in! You're outta here.
You passed! You failed.

The difference between someone described as "out of this world" and someone you can't wait to get out of your world is class. You might immediately consider appearance in deciding if someone's got class. But a person can *look* sharp and still be a jerk. Class is not all manners either. People can act prim and proper and, in the end, that's all it is – an act. Finally, class is not about being cool. Some are so cool they are cold to everyone but those in certain cliques.

So what is class? Class is a state of being that starts on the inside and shows up on the outside. My mentor always said you could spot it by the way a person enters a room. Some walk in with a "Look! Here I am!" versus an "Ah, there *you* are" attitude.

Class reminds me of diamonds – not baseball or softball diamonds, sports fans, but those sparkly rocks most girls eventually want. The word evokes notions of style, elegance, beauty, lasting value (and the need for a fat savings account). Believe it or not, a lifetime of developing class can be compared to how a diamond forms over millions of years.

They rise up. Diamonds start hardening deep within the Earth and then rise to the top. Class happens the same way, deep inside. As it rises to the surface, you will sparkle and shine next to the rough rocks and dull stones around you.

They form under pressure. It takes intense pressure to create a diamond. Class often emerges under the same conditions. Imagine your first big job interview or dining with your girlfriend's parents and discovering her dad stands 6'4" and weighs 300 pounds. Consider moving to a new school during your senior year. How would winning or losing the biggest game of the season change you? What would you do if you got dumped by your dream date? How you handle moments like these will show your class or lack of it.

They reflect variety. Diamonds come in all shapes, sizes and colors – including pink and blue. In the same way, class can surface in anyone. You don't have to be rich or drop-dead gorgeous to be classy. Class threads through every heritage, every personality and every age. It is waiting to show up in you.

They hold up. As the hardest known natural substance, diamonds are durable and versatile. They both sparkle as expensive jewelry and cut through just about anything as a saw blade. Similarly, class can help you find something to smile about in the midst of tough times and can slice through bad attitudes and bad mouthing like nothing else.

They are rare. No one stumbles upon diamonds during the family camping trip. Rather, these rare rocks must be unearthed with maximum effort – by mining, digging or blasting. Finding the stone is just the first step. One diamond karat might exist in 100 tons of mud. So, freeing the diamond's truest beauty involves cleaning, cutting and polishing. Class calls for the same. In this case, the "mud" that needs to go might be your temptation to cheat, gossip, break hearts or brown nose.

They must be genuine. Many have tried to pass off fake diamonds as the real deal. Some artificial diamonds might look strikingly similar to the real thing, but they cannot withstand much testing. They chip and crack under stress.

They need polishing. Over time, dirt, body oil and everyday wear can make a diamond look dull. However, the fire and brilliance will return with some polishing. So it goes with class. When you dabble in the "mud" discussed earlier – behaviors that typically don't bring out your best – you might lose some shine. But that change does not have to be a permanent one.

Okay, the geology lesson is over, and it is now time to dig for some class and learn how to polish it.

Actions speak loudest. Studies show in a face-to-face meeting, body language sends 55 percent of your message, tone of voice 38 percent and actual words just 7 percent. What you say is not nearly as important as how you say it. To get your message across with more class and clarity, consider the following body language pointers:

- *Say cheese!* People with class know that smiling – the universal expression of friendly greeting and good will – means even more to someone feeling tired or stressed. Yet, many people look tired, mad, frustrated or upset when they let their face relax. If smiling often feels like a strain, focus on maintaining a pleasant facial expression. Think about something that makes you feel happy, something that will put a twinkle in your eye and cause your cheeks to naturally flex.
- *Make eye contact.* Looking someone in the eye communicates two things – that you want to be in conversation with them and that they can trust you. However, good eye contact stops short of a staring or "no blink" contest.
- *Stop fidgeting.* Fidgeting is a sign of nervousness and often distracts.
- *Keep arms at sides.* Avoid the "fig leaf" look – folding your hands in front or behind you as if you were naked and trying to cover up. Remember, eyes go where your hands go. Do you really want others looking there?
- *Don't flip out.* People who flip their hair call attention to themselves. People with class call attention to others. Leave hair and accessories alone. Set it and forget it!
- *Lean forward.* This simple move communicates that you are interested and focused on what someone else is saying.

- *Lean back.* When the conversation becomes more comfortable, lean back to show that you are relaxed and open. Note, however, that leaning back too far could send another message – that you feel bored.

- *Uncross your arms.* Arms folded across your chest signals that you might be closed to what another is saying.

- *Share the air.* While others may be eager to hear your stories, talking non-stop is rude. Yet, sometimes even classy people forget to listen. By listening well, you let others know that you consider them important.

- *Remain positive.* Class acts avoid gossiping and complaining. They do not use negative body language, a harsh tone of voice or abusive words. When you need to share something negative – and there will be times – do it in a positive way. A positive attitude creates a domino effect. Others will eventually follow your lead.

Host with the Most! People with class often aim to make others feel welcome, connected and important – even if it's not their party! How?

- *Practice the ABCs.* Always be caring. Always be comforting. Always be connecting.

- *Never greet from your seat.* Always stand up. This is a powerful way to acknowledge and include others. Also, always give up your seat to an older person – no questions asked.

- *Practice delivering a confident handshake.* A simple handshake tells volumes. To make the best impression, extend your right arm, make an open landing spot with your hand, grip the other person's hand firmly so that the mesh between your thumb and first finger meet and shake two to three times.

- *Search for wallflowers.* Find that lonely guy pasted against the wall or the lady lost in the crowd. Reach out by striking up a conversation.
- *Break the ice.* Consider awkward times when no one knows each other or what to say next as your golden opportunity! Start by saying, "hello." Shake hands. Ask a question. Reflect out loud on something unique about the atmosphere or event. Breaking the ice means finding the common ground needed to connect with others.

Wise Words. The root word of communication is "commune," which means to bring together. People with class are masters at communicating to this end. These tools can help you do the same:

- *Word of the week.* Select at least one underused word every week and add it to your vocabulary. Try using "delight" instead of "happy" or "remarkable" instead of "great." However, remember that sticking with this exercise doesn't mean you need to morph into a walking SAT study guide.
- *Stop cursing.* Everyone, from TV characters to ten-year-olds, seems to be cursing more. One of my first girl friends – a class act – told me after I cursed once that she considered cursing a sign of a weak vocabulary and a weak mind. I didn't make that mistake again.

- *Ditch filler words.* Get rid of old standbys – *um, and, stuff, things, ya know* and *like*. Though they easily slip into conversations, they are terribly annoying and unfitting for someone with class. If you can't think of a word, slow your speaking, pause and think before going on. You'll speak with more authority.

- *Bag the negative.* Certain words have no business in the language of classy people. Remove "problem" from your vocabulary. Unless you are on a space ship and you're calling Houston to get help, you don't have a problem. That word makes a situation seem unsolvable, and classy people rarely accept unsolvable situations. Use "challenge" or "concern" or "special circumstance" instead.

Thanksgiving and Celebration. The essence of class comes from showing appreciation and respect for others. People with class know that they never accomplish goals independently. So, seek to celebrate your heroes rather than hog the spotlight. Be humble in receiving recognition and generous in sharing praise. Here are some keys to expressing gratitude:

- *Write it.* E-mail is better than nothing, but a traditional handwritten note is best!

- *Point out specifics.* Specifying what you appreciate shows that you have noticed someone's effort and understand what it means.

- *Respond promptly.* Make haste to share your thanks! Keep a stack of notes handy to make a quick response convenient. This need not become a chore. Rather, it's a chance to show you care.

- *Praise publicly.* Recognizing someone publicly is one of the most powerful ways to show appreciation. This can inspire others to seek excellence.

- *Graciously accept praise.* Milking compliments by talking about the tough assignment or the unbelievable obstacles you needed to overcome to succeed lacks class. Politely say "thank you" when others praise you.

Bon Appetite. As you get older, dining situations will become more critical to your personal and professional success. Class can shine in these settings with some etiquette basics:

- *Never call attention to yourself.* Don't talk with your mouth full, scarf food or overstuff yourself – even if it is your favorite meal. Take small bites, and cut the food in bite-sized pieces as you eat versus all at once. Serve others first. Avoid ordering notoriously messy-to-eat foods. Elbows off the table! Squelch any complaints about the food and how your mom makes it better.

- *Network.* Sharing a meal gives you another opportunity to connect. Ask questions. Reflect on positive news. Explore interesting information.

- *Nourishment is optional.* If you leave a meal hungry because the conversation was so tasty, great! The experience should be richer than what is on the plate.

On the Catwalk. For better and for worse, people will judge the amount of class you've got by what you wear. Follow these basic tips to dress up:

- *Go pressed & polished.* People notice scuffed shoes, wrinkled clothes and poorly fitted attire for all the wrong reasons. A pressed look shows you pay attention to detail, which can make a big difference in many areas. By the way, tuck in your shirt and pull up your pants.

- *Ask what grandma would say.* While a wide range of dress is permissible, submit yourself to the "Gram Test" to send the most respectable message. Would she let you out of the house looking like that? While her standard may seem outdated and conservative, it's safe! You won't offend others, especially elders.

- *Touch up with make-up.* This does not mean single-handedly bumping the profitability of cosmetics companies. Some women over do it. However, applying some blush, eye shadow and a little lipstick can help you look more put together.

- *Accessorize!* Remember that small posts – no more than two per ear, please – often top dangly earrings in the class category. In professional settings, remove accessories from the tongue, nose, eyebrows, etc. Limit rings to no more than two per hand. Gentlemen, your belt should match your shoes.

- *Spray the scent of success.* Perfume or cologne and deodorant are a must – in small amounts. Appealing to the senses in this way encourages others to create more pleasant memories of you. However, they should not be able to sniff you before they meet you!

These suggestions can help your class rise to the top. Remember, class is not an act, it is who you are! Class is how your inner character is displayed to the world.

Former UCLA basketball coach John Wooden said it best, "Be more concerned with your character than your reputation. Your character is who you really are while your reputation is who others think you are."

Ideally, your class, character, and reputation will be mirror images. In a world of rocks and stones, be a diamond. As you rise to the top, you'll bring others with you!

ABOUT THE AUTHOR

Ryan Underwood

Ryan is the Chief Leadership Officer of TRI Leadership Resources. He is dedicated to the principle that making a difference everyday equals a lifetime of MADness! He lives this each day as a trainer and personal coach to leaders of national student organizations (FBLA, DECA, HOSA, FCCLA, TSA, student government). He is a consultant with clients ranging from Disney and March of Dimes to schools, universities, and state departments of education. Ryan is a speaker, co-author of the "EXTRA STEP," architect of national leadership achievement programs, and a believer that everyday is an opportunity to make a positive impact.

Ryan Underwood
TRI Leadership Resources, LLC
P.O. Box 912
Jacksonville, OR 97530
Office: 714-730-5999 Fax: 714-730-7922
Toll Free: 888-786-7526
Email: ryan@teamtri.com
Web Site: www.trileadership.com

CHRIS BOWERS

Making a Difference One Person at a Time

CHAPTER

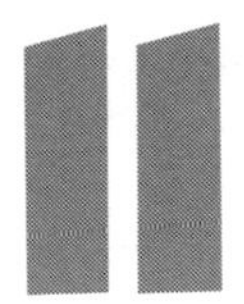

Making a Difference One Person at a Time

Chris Bowers

The last night Chad turned in for bed was a cold and snowy one. Yet, as he slept, a hot blaze began raging through his house. When the fireman pulled him from the flames alive, approximately 75 of us gathered outside the hospital emergency room hoping to witness a miracle. If anyone deserved one, it was Chad.

We didn't get our miracle.

That afternoon, at 4 p.m., January 21, 1995, the doctors switched Chad's life support machines off. The smoke had blackened his lungs, and this circle of friends next met at his funeral along with hundreds of other mourners. Though each remembered something different about Chad, they had more than grief in common. They all recognized how this one person had made a big difference in all of their lives.

Chad never led a revolution or joined the Peace Corps. His face never graced a baseball card or a box of cereal. The 21-year-old frat boy never governed a state or closed big business deals. But the procession from the funeral home to the cemetery took 45 minutes to pass and stretched nearly three miles.

Why? Chad sought out those who needed encouragement and encouraged them. He looked for people who needed praise and praised them. He found people who needed comfort and comforted them. He realized that everyone needed love, and he loved them. Even in death, he gave life to five or six strangers through various organ donations.

For better and for worse, funerals give survivors a chance to reminisce about the kind of life the deceased's lived. What will others say about you? Will your memory call to mind positive or negative experiences?

Though Chad's life ended tragically and much too soon, recounting stories from a few of those who paid their respects beside his casket might shed light on how you, too, can make a difference – one person at a time.

Me

I met Chad in the no parking zone in front of my dormitory during my first day on campus as a college freshman. Instead of flipping the hazard lights on there and taking armloads of stuff up to my new room one trip at a time, the resident directors told me to pile it all on the sidewalk and park at the stadium a mile away.

Everyone else who pulled up with an overstuffed car had a parent in tow, someone who could watch their belongings while they ditched the family sedan. But not me. I had been way too cool to let my parents tag along with me to school.

So, since I arrived alone, I started arguing with the staff for not letting me move in right then and there.

Chad overheard me quarreling and stepped into help, ASAP. I figured he was a sophomore officially in charge of moving people like me in because he watched my mountain of unpacked stuff and then joined me for the next hour in schlepping it to my room on the 8th floor.

Eventually, however, I realized that Chad was a freshman, just like me, and that he had pitched in to move my things before moving his own. I had never met someone so ready to help others before. That's how our great friendship started.

Still, we used to argue all the time, which wasn't that unusual for me. Back then, I was a know-it-all kind of guy. Once I formed an opinion, which was instantly, it didn't matter what anyone else said. I wouldn't change my mind, and for this reason, people didn't like me very much. But ten minutes into one of the many heated, no-win conversations I shared with Chad, he said something that changed my life forever.

"Bowers, have you ever shut up for five minutes and listened to what anyone else has had to say?" he asked.

I paused. Had I ever shut up long enough to listen to anybody? No. I was so in love with the sound of my voice, that I never heard anyone else's. But after that confrontation, I spent the next hour and a half listening as Chad explained that if I wanted people to like me, I had to like them first. I had to listen to their ideas, and give them praise when they deserved it. I had to let them know that they were worth listening to, because everyone is important.

I think about Chad's words to me that day years ago all the time.

Tim

When I met Tim for the first time at Chad's funeral, he explained that he was the oldest child in a poor, makeshift family living on the outskirts of a ghetto. Because his father had disappeared early on, and his mother worked so much, Tim got very little encouragement. Consequently, by the seventh grade he hated school, hated life and had all but given up.

He hooked up with Chad when the high school-sponsored mentoring program hosted an event for him and 50 other at-risk seventh graders. Tim remembered half-heartedly participating that first day and mostly ignoring Chad when he spoke. But by the next event, his attitude had dramatically changed due to some unexpected one-on-one time with Chad.

Tim had been shuffling down the street after school and minding his own business when the two crossed paths. Tim recognized Chad, but had no intention of saying a word. He didn't need to.

"Hey Tim! How are you?" Chad asked. Tim told me that it was the first time an older student had ever remembered his name. Instead of responding to the friendly greeting, Tim said he fired back a question.

"How do you remember my name?" Tim said to the high school mentor. That's when Chad did what Chad always did. He seized the unexpected opportunity to make a difference in someone else's life. In this case, he told Tim that he noticed him for the way he had shared some good ideas with the group and gotten them to listen. Chad said he recognized leadership qualities in Tim.

That was it. The interaction between the high school mentor and the troubled middle school student lasted less than five minutes. They exchanged only a few sentences, but those rare words of encouragement caught Tim's attention. When Chad returned to the middle school to mentor, Tim felt excited. Instead of seeing Chad as another teacher, he saw him as an ally – even as a friend.

Over time, Chad convinced Tim to join the student council and try out for the basketball team. With steady encouragement from a role model, the lonely, sad kid with no hope blossomed into the leader that Chad said he could be. Instead of joining a gang, Tim contemplated running for class president. When Chad died that January, Tim was class president of his senior class and a leader on the school's basketball team.

Emily

I also met Emily, a former restaurant co-worker of Chad's, at his funeral. She was a high school senior earning "okay" grades during their shared work stint. But she confessed to Chad that she doubted she had what it would take to make it in college. She explained that she was afraid – afraid that she wasn't good enough, afraid of putting financial strain on her parents and afraid to dream.

Instead of accepting that self-assessment, Chad arrived at the restaurant the next day with a pile of college information for Emily. His arms were full of applications from four area colleges, a book on college shopping along with scholarship and financial aid paperwork.

Every time business slowed at the restaurant, Chad helped Emily with the long application process. He helped her every step of the way, she said. That paid off when she got accepted and landed enough financial aid to afford to enroll.

Instead of letting that friendship wither when she went off to school, Chad kept in touch. He called her every month or so just to see how things were going. When she got stressed out, she called him because he always made her feel like she could make it. With his support, she not only passed her classes, she made the dean's list.

Justin

When Justin joined our fraternity as a freshman, his social life looked bleak. He ate alone in the dining hall, played video games solo most of the day and had never gone out on a date. But Justin was just the kind of guy Chad looked for, someone who needed a break.

So, as a bunch of us upperclassmen headed off to the dining hall one night, Chad invited Justin along. He told us ahead of time about his plan – to laugh at everything this goofy geek said – in order to build his confidence. Chad explained that if we reacted positively to him, he might start to like himself more and get along with everyone better.

It wasn't easy, but we followed Chad's directions. Every time Justin cracked a joke, funny or not, we laughed like he was Seinfeld. Sure enough, by the meal's end, Justin walked a little taller and had even gotten funnier – for real.

Though his conversational awkwardness began disappearing, Justin's wardrobe lingered. So, Chad waded into his closet and yanked certain items he said should never ever be worn in public again. Later, Chad took Justin shopping for replacement duds. But throughout the process, he stopped short of making fun. He never put him down, just pumped him up.

Chad also taught Justin some tips on wooing women. He explained the importance of maintaining good eye contact, smiling, complimenting them on their hair or shoes and in general showering them with enough attention so they feel like the center of attention at all times. Chad also passed along the most important rule. Rule number one states that if you put your arm around a girl, and she doesn't put her arm around you, LET GO!

By the time rush week arrived, Justin had morphed into a pretty cool guy. But it wasn't the new clothes. It was his new confidence. Since we didn't treat him like a geek, he didn't feel like one or carry himself like one either. Eighteen months later, Justin had made plenty of friends and had a pretty girlfriend.

What Can You Do?

- **Identify the needy**. Every person needs some help at one time or another. Look for those who need something you have. If you are a terrible basketball player, coaching someone on their jump shot might not be super helpful. However, if you are a senior with lots of friends, you could reach out to a shy freshman with lousy people skills. By matching your abilities and interests with a person struggling in that area, you can make a huge difference.

Could you encourage a depressed kid like Tim? Do you have a friend like Emily who needs self-confidence to follow their dreams? Can you find someone like Justin who needs to know he is worthwhile and can fit in?

- **Truly care**. You can't make the most difference if you reach out only to look like a good person or feel better about your position in life. Instead, you must really care about the person you are trying to help. Nobody wants to be used or patronized.

- **Determine what, exactly, is needed**. Have you ever walked into a barbershop or salon and specifically described the haircut you want only to walk out with something altogether different? The problem happens when you tell the stylist what you want – what you think would look good – and that person instead snips according to their vision for your hairdo.

  If you want to make a positive difference, listen carefully. Don't assume you know what someone else needs. Avoid pushing your priorities into someone else's life. You can council and give advice, but make sure you are trying to meet their needs, not yours.

- **Offer genuine friendship.** Friendship usually paves the way for more open communication. So, if you take a freshman under your wing, launch the relationship by explaining why you want to be friends before outlining why they need your support. Then, be patient. By taking enough time to build trust, you will eventually get that person to stop buttoning their shirt up to their chin and tucking their jeans down to their ankles.

- **Follow up**. The only thing worse than missing the chance to be someone's pet project is, after a brief season of mentoring, getting tossed like last year's Capri pants. To make a difference in some else's life now and for years to come, be there for the long haul. If you are looking for a quick fix, go rake an old lady's yard or start a canned food drive. Both noble endeavors will give you a sense of giving back without requiring any long-term commitment. However, if you follow the first four steps, living a legacy like the one Chad left will be a snap. Why not get started today?

ABOUT THE AUTHOR

Chris Bowers

In high school and college, Chris began speaking in front of audiences such as Student Councils, Key Clubs, and Hugh O'Brian. He graduated from Ball State University with a Bachelor of Arts in Political Science. In 1996, he began his professional speaking career and has appeared as the keynote speaker at many state and regional conferences and in over one hundred middle schools and high schools.

Chris speaks to audiences about the power they have to take risks and to have confidence in themselves. He uses humor to encourage them to overcome their fear of what others may think of them.

Bowers Success Development
1233 E. 61st St.
Indianapolis, IN 46220
317-201-5583
Email:motive8u@aol.com
Web Site:www.wireinthenose.com

STU SAUNDERS

Knock, Knock... Who's There?

CHAPTER

12

Knock, Knock... Who's There?

Stu Saunders

The whole point of this book is to figure out how to make the world around you a better place. But you may figure that you'll never be able to crack the code since the world is so big and you are so small next to it.

"I'm just a kid in high school," you might be thinking. "What can I possibly do?"

Lots! It starts with learning to listen more closely for opportunity knocking – even when it seems like there's no door to answer.

I never made the dean's list or the honor roll. But after attending a college for broadcasting and communication, I landed a job working at a radio station in London, Ontario. Radio 1290 CJBK was an "oldies" format and far from being the hippest frequency in my hometown. Nonetheless, I was proud to be a disk jockey and very excited to move one step closer to my dream job of being the morning man on a hot station in Toronto or Vancouver.

But my beginnings in this business could not have been more glamour-free. I worked from midnight to 6 a.m. playing the "Dick Bartley Rock-and-Roll Oldies Show" and commercials during Blue Jay games. Because the station paid squat, I had to wait tables at a local restaurant and sell products for a screen-printing company just to keep food on the table and a roof over my head.

Yet, opportunity often knocks when you least expect it. That's what happened one evening as I attended a meeting for various high school student council officers. I showed up to pitch a new line of t-shirts for the screen-printing company, but the students were more interested in complaining about no-show officers.

In frustration, they turned to me for answers. How could they remedy the absenteeism? I folded my shirts and suggested that they invite leaders from all of the area schools to a daylong conference designed to promote the benefits of getting involved in an area-wide student council group.

The idea instantly caught on. Minutes later, I sensed opportunity knocking when they started brainstorming about booking a speaker. They asked me if I had any suggestions.

"I can do it!" I said. "Give me a shot!"

Before long, I was standing before 150 student leaders as a keynote speaker. Since that day in 1991 when I launched my career, speaking jobs have brought me to more than 40 states, every Canadian province and the Yukon Territory. However, had I not dropped my t-shirt pitch to pursue the speaking opportunity, may be I'd still be juggling three jobs – playing commercials on some lame radio station, waiting tables and selling t-shirts.

Instead, I decided to open myself to new ideas and new directions. I heard the knock and answered. Many students, on the other hand, get so caught up in day-to-day worries that revolve around achieving the right look, hanging out with the right friends and listening to the right music that they forget to focus on seizing the right opportunities when they come along.

To recognize and respond to the great opportunities that might come your way, consider the following.

Decide what you want to accomplish.

Drop everything right now to scribble down your dreams. What do you most want to accomplish? Don't let the lack of time, money or skills block your train of thought. Play some upbeat music and let your imagination run free. Keep jamming on your list for at least 30 nonstop minutes. Relax! There are no wrong answers.

When finished, give yourself a high five! You have at last captured some cool ideas and hidden dreams on paper. Surprised? Had you ever considered becoming CEO of a major company or the star quarterback of the Dallas Cowboys? You may want to paint or sing or stay home and rear a family. Life is full of possibilities!

Appraise your situation today.

How can you get to where you want to be if you don't know where you are now?

For the first seven years of my speaking career I traveled with a talented speaking partner – Andrew Thibodeau. As high school classmates, I would never have pictured this partnership because Andy and I ran in completely different circles. His friends considered student leadership types like me "geeks" and "losers." They constantly cracked jokes and were nothing but rude to us during assemblies and pep rallies.

So, when a teacher invited Andy to join student council, his friends discouraged him. That pressure could have kept Andy from answering the door. He could have laughed off the opportunity. He instead joined, and we quickly became friends.

Though we goofed off a lot, we took student leadership seriously – something that helped make our friendship a lasting one. Taking this student leadership opportunity together eventually provided the bedrock for our shared career in encouraging youth.

Remember that taking one opportunity can lead to many others. For instance, Andy and I both met our significant others when we were on the road for speaking engagements.

Seeing and seizing opportunities now doesn't necessarily mean dumping your friends. Just make absolutely certain that those "friends" don't try plugging your ears to opportunity's knock.

Keep and open mind.

Don't wait to follow someone else's lead to do something big! You can expect opportunity to knock, and you will be able to open the door – if you live each day with an open mind.

When I was in high school, one of my classmates witnessed his house going up in flames. The blaze destroyed his home and most of the family's belongings. Without homeowner's insurance, that family's situation seemed hopeless.

But I recognized that amid the ashes there was an opportunity. After rallying a couple of friends, we launched a fundraising campaign and raised more than $10,000 – something that made a huge difference in the lives of those five people.

Together, we heard opportunity knocking. We could have closed our minds to the possibilities and given the family nothing more than sympathy. Instead, we opened the door and found a way to make a real difference. By promoting a school dance, a bake sale and a "kiss the pig" competition, we had fun and spared the family from becoming homeless.

Opportunities of this magnitude may be just around the corner for you, too. Some doors might slam in your face. Not all opportunities lead to positive results. However, remember that when things don't go as planned, you must get back up, brush yourself off and try again.

Regardless of the outcome, I have found that there's always joy in opening up to possibilities, be it helping a child in need or starting a recycling effort in your school. Who knows? One thing is for sure. Someone needs you and your resources right now. Look around. The possibilities are endless and the rewards are the sweetest you'll ever experience!

Oh, what's that I hear?

Something is knocking at my door. I'd better go answer it.

"Hello?!?"

ABOUT THE AUTHOR

Stu Saunders

Stu Saunders is a former radio broadcaster who since early 1992, at age 22, developed a career delivering motivational presentations and leadership workshops across North America. As of 2003 he has made more than 1700 appearances in all ten Canadian provinces and over forty US states. His program has reached well over 1,000,000 youth across North America.

Through his Company, Leadership Innovations, Stu organizes an international summer leadership camp called Youth Leadership Camps Canada that has reached over 2000 youth from 17 different countries. In 1999, he became the coordinator of the second-largest youth leadership conference in Canada. Stu has made a full time commitment to helping others reach their goals and dreams.

Stu Saunders • Leadership Innovations Inc.
585 Eden Ave
London, Ontario, Canada, N6C 2Z5
Office: 519-438-4800 Fax: 519-438-1930
Email: stu@ylcc.com
Web Site: www.leadershipinnovations.com

AARON FOSTER

You Can End or Begin Your Life in Seconds!

CHAPTER

13

You Can End or Begin Your Life in Seconds!

Aaron Foster

My best friend was a likable enough guy and, for a time, he was very involved in the world around him. He participated in sports, chorus, orchestra, drama and student council. He studied for tests and did well. He loved his supportive family. But he was chubby, and that negative aspect of his life eventually blocked him from considering any of these positives.

Somewhere during the 7th and 8th grade, classmates started calling him the fat kid. In this way, he went from being the last picked for elementary school recess games to a sitting duck target for bullies in junior high.

The older he got, the more weight he gained, and his life at school soon became unbearably stressful. But instead of getting help and tackling the troubled areas, he made his way to the bathroom medicine cabinet and swallowed 17 Tylenol pills. Late that night, he thought he was pulling the covers to his chin for the last time.

When he woke the next morning, he felt even more defeated than he had the night before for failing in his desperate mission. Still, he managed to continue his normal routine without telling a soul about the pills or his painful daily experience. He instead put on his "school attitude" – the carefree face he hid behind at school while he secretly suffered ever-darker moods.

Not surprisingly, a few months later, my friend trekked to the medicine cabinet again and downed 46 pills before heading off to bed. He felt sick the next morning, but he had survived the overdose.

This second private failure took place during what adults recognize as a bumpy time, those ultra awkward junior high years. Though miserable then, this hefty guy dreaded ninth grade more. He was convinced the bigger classes and tougher kids would make his life even more of a living hell. While he worried about that grim future, his grades slipped. Still, he stayed as active as ever in extracurricular activities to camouflage his misery from those who could not read his report card.

This kid had so much going for him – he just didn't know it. So, when life at school next overwhelmed him, he decided to get serious. He discarded thoughts of popping even more pills in favor of picking up a 9mm handgun. He told an older friend that he needed to borrow the gun to shoot small game, and the friend believed him.

With the lethal weapon in hand, he sank into a recliner in the family living room one dreary Tuesday in November. No one was home, and the house seemed to hold its breath as he contemplated the next moments.

Tears streamed down the young man's face as he thought about who and what he would miss by ending it all. Yet, the emotional pain he felt outweighed those thoughts. He leaned back in the recliner, slowly lifted the loaded 9mm pistol and placed the cool nozzle on his right temple.

After a simple count to five, he resigned to shoot. His finger firmly curled around the trigger and he began counting out loud in the quiet room. He let a long pause hang between each number while his eyes gushed and his nose ran.

"One ... Two ... Three ... Four ... " he said sadly. But just before he pronounced "Five," a voice floated through his head.

"You can either blow your head off and end it all now," it whispered. "Or, you can set the gun down, get off your butt and make the most out of your life." That voice made him sniffle, wipe his face and wait a minute. Visions of all the cruel kids that had mercilessly teased him came to mind, and suddenly he wanted to show them what he was made of more than he wanted to kill himself.

The reason I know that friend's situation so well is because *it was me!*

That was the scariest day of my life – a day when split-second decisions never meant more. But, for me, it took getting to the end of a loaded gun before I realized that I could take charge of my life, that I could make better decisions about how to manage stress and make it through tough times.

Getting a grip began with writing an honest evaluation. For starters, I drew a line down the middle of a blank piece of paper. On the left side of the page I listed all the negatives in my life. On the other side, I listed all the positives.

Of course the negative side of the page was packed full of everything. On the positive side, I could count only a couple of things.

When I put the pencil down, I ripped off the side that listed the negative things, crumpled it into a ball and made a free throw with it to the wastebasket. Then I put my chin on my folded hands and just stared at the short list of positives.

What did I most want to do with my life, now that I still had it?

I had no clue. At the time, my strongest impulses involved taking out a strange form of revenge on those who had taunted me to the brink of my very existence. I wanted to show every last one of them that I wouldn't be eating dirt on the ground for long. I was more than just FAT! That was, I realized, the only thing they saw then.

Despite the general drive to retaliate, I noticed a couple of other things that made me reconsider my worth. I had written that I was a people person, a music lover and someone who wanted to own his own business. I figured that focusing on a combination all three would sooner or later open a door to some new opportunities if I thought long and hard enough about the possibilities.

Ultimately, I kept coming up with the idea of starting a disc jockey company. It didn't faze me that the majority of small business owners have long since graduated from high school. I was 15 years old then, and I figured it was a great time to get busy.

My plan worked! I made $20,000 during those high school years. I stuck with it five years after I walked out of there with a diploma and managed to grow the business from 37 events a year to 167 before retiring in my mid 20s when I got tired of working weekends.

In the meantime, though, people were blown away that I was successful enough to DJ full time and earn a decent living. I got extra recognition when industry magazines and websites profiled my success story as a young entrepreneur in the biz. I later got an opportunity to be one of the youngest keynote speakers at a national industry convention.

Looking back, I realize I would never have tasted those sweet successes had I not put the gun down to set some goals. Without goals to motivate me, I may have become indefinitely mired in depression or found rest in a pine box 6 feet under.

If you only get one thing out of this chapter let it be this. *Don't try going through life without setting goals!* People without clearly defined goals often wind up like cats – chasing their tails and going nowhere.

Once you achieve your first round of goals, be sure to set more. If at any time your goals seem like a bad fit with your interests and abilities, then erase them and write new ones that are more achievable.

Though I started setting goals at age 15 to crawl out of the dark and dangerous pit I found myself in, as an adult I still set goals as a matter of habit. One of my more recent goals involved losing weight. Given all the grief I've encountered because of my size, it was always in the back of my mind to shed my extra pounds. But given the goal – losing 160 lbs, which is a little less than half of me at average weight – it took some time to get into the right mindset.

First, I determined that I couldn't attempt this difficult a goal to please anyone else. I didn't want to do it so I could have the MTV look or so that I could pick up more girls. I knew the best motivation would need to come from within. So, I focused on the health concerns that were facing me then and also in the future. For instance, asthma and a high cholesterol count plagued me and many other people who struggle with being overweight.

To get down to my ideal weight, I remember a practice that had helped me achieve goals, no matter how difficult they at first seemed. So, for seven months, I celebrated! I celebrated the small steps that would eventually get me to my goal. By recognizing the baby steps, I slowly but surely did it.

After eight months, I lost the other person in me – nearly 170 pounds! Friends, family and co-workers couldn't believe the visible change taking place and neither could I! All I know is the power of goal setting and celebrating every victory, big or small, in that direction.

For you, the goal might have nothing to do with getting the bathroom scale's needle to inch toward the left. Maybe it's earning a 3.2 grade point average or higher during the next semester.

CELEBRATE!

It could be making it to church every week.

CELEBRATE!

Perhaps it will be practicing your sport during the off-season for at least 45 minutes every day or getting five blue ribbons at the county fair.

CELEBRATE!

The more time you take to celebrate the small things, the more often the big things will happen. On the other hand, there is nothing more dangerous than someone who gives up and drops his or her goals. This is a red flag for nearly everyone struggling with suicidal thoughts.

When I was suicidal, I had abandoned all of my goals. But when at the last minute I saw the light, when I realized the power of goal setting, it changed my near deadly circumstances into something a whole lot better.

But you don't have to be suicidal to greatly benefit from the discipline of goal setting. To live a more fulfilling life, consider the following:

- **Settle old scores.** Have you recently teased, bullied or fought with someone? No matter how unthinkable, getting right with a person you've wronged is often a key to living a happier, healthier life. Find that person and apologize. Don't spend too much time talking about the past. Talk about the future instead. Go hang out with that person. Go to lunch with them. Go shopping with them. Make sure they know you appreciate them, and that you are real. Investing in a friendship and building trust between you will pay off with peace of mind.

- **Set goals.** Make a list of 5 goals that you would like to accomplish in the next 6 months. Make sure that they are achievable! Don't write down a goal to make it on next year's basketball team when maybe the tryouts are 10 months away. Think short term, and remember to CELEBRATE each baby step along the way!

- **Reach out.** If you or a friend are suicidal and need help, reach out immediately. Talk to trusted adults – family members, school counselors, or somebody else who you know cares. If you feel uncomfortable sharing your suicidal thoughts with someone you know, call 1-800-SUICIDE for confidential counseling.

- **Support suicide prevention.** Prevention is the key to putting a stop to suicide. Step out and be the leader. Gather a group of people in your school or community and start a Yellow Ribbon chapter. Your Yellow Ribbon chapter would be in charge of creating suicide awareness within your school and community. This is a great way to get the word out about how suicide can effect everyone. For more information, visit www.yellowribbon.org

ABOUT THE AUTHOR

Aaron Foster

Though a Boone, Iowa, native, Aaron Foster now lives in Kansas City Missouri – home base for his career as a national motivational youth speaker. His topic specialties include suicide prevention, teen violence, leadership and goal setting.

Foster most often presents to students at middle schools, high schools and colleges. However, he also offers staff development programs and speaks at parent and community forums. Besides speaking, he has served as a church youth director and youth sports coach.

His hobbies include playing sports, coaching and officiating high school sports, volunteering with various organizations, going to church and playing golf!

Aaron Foster
Big Star Productions
PO Box 10730, Gladstone, MO 64188-0730
816-436-1911
Toll Free: 888-537-4320
Email: bigdesk@aaronfoster.com
Web Site: www.aaronfoster.com

RAY LOZANO

"Fear-less" Factor

CHAPTER

14

"Fear-less" Factor

Ray Lozano

Dan, 42, St. Louis, Missouri –
"I had a fear of trying out for football, so I didn't. I look back and regret that I never went for it. Now I've forgotten the excuses, but I definitely remember the feeling of not trying out for the team."

Rebecca, 23, Dallas, Texas –
"I had an opportunity to bike through Europe with my friends during the summer between high school and college. I was afraid that I wouldn't be able to finish. My friends encouraged me, but I chose to work. Now I regret not trying as my friends had a really great time and I missed out on an experience of a lifetime."

Keshia, 36, San Bernardino, California –
"I love little kids. My friends tell me I should open a childcare center but I'm afraid that I wouldn't succeed. What if I didn't get enough kids? So I spend my time dreaming about it, knowing that if I did

open my own place, it would be the most wonderful in the world for children."

Carla, 19, Little Rock, Arkansas –
"When I was in high school I was really afraid to try out for the cheerleading squad. Every time I thought of auditioning, my stomach did flips. Looking back, I'm really sad that I never took the chance."

Fear of failure. Fear of ridicule. Fear of being too insignificant to make a difference. Fear stopped these people from doing what they wanted to do. Is fear standing between you and what you really want to accomplish?

Not surprisingly, fear can immobilize you and keep you from pursuing your potential – even though many fears are not based in fact. Still, it doesn't matter *why* you give up. It only matters that you *have* given up. To press on, remember that facing your fear is a lot like fighting a giant made out of crackers. From a distance, it may appear huge. It might seem even more gigantic as you get closer. But if you're bold enough to attack it, you could buzz right through and reduce it to a pile of crumbs.

Of course, not everyone is afraid of the same things. There are literally hundreds of different documented phobias (types of fears). The names alone can crack you up! Check these out:

Alektorophobia – The fear of chickens

Geliophobia – stop reading if you have this; it's the fear of laughter.

Xanthophobia – The fear of the color yellow. (Watch out corn!)

Glossphobia – The fear of speaking in public.

Pupaphobia – The fear of puppets.

Arachnophobia – The fear of spiders.

Emetophobia – The fear of vomiting.

Wakenphobia – The fear of having to get up early for school. (Okay, I made that one up. But if it did exist, I bet I had it as a kid!)

Can you imagine if you had the dreaded Alektor-Xantho-Emeto-Pupaphobia? You would fear being chased by a chicken with a yellow beak while barfing on a puppet. Though absurd, this illustrates the power of fear – whatever the type – to provoke change. Whether that fear paralyzes or motivates depends on your approach.

To turn fear into a positive motivator, picture it as a large wall. As you approach, you see the scary side. That side will send you running. Graffiti such as "loser" and "wimp" and other phrases that read "You aren't good enough" and "You're going to look like a fool!" cover that side. If you stand before that wall long enough, those words will echo in your mind and intimidate you from even trying to get over it.

You're frozen if you try scaling a wall of fear with this perspective. Sure, it looks like it's made of iron and bricks, and it appears to be too high to hurdle. With that impression, no wonder people facing the wall quickly decide to head down another path, even though that path eventually leads to a land of regret and missed opportunities. But from another vantage point, you could see the truth – that this seemingly impenetrable wall is just a thin sheet of tissue paper.

I remember turning away from a tissue paper wall on several occasions. One of my earliest recollections took place at the fair when I was just a kid. All my friends wanted to ride "The Death Drop" except me. I think it was the ride's name that paralyzed me with fear. Death meant dying, and drop meant falling. Why wouldn't I interpret that name to really mean "fall to your death"? If the ride had been called "The Gentle Nudge," I would have chanced it. Instead, I waited in line with my buddies for 18 minutes only to bail out with a flimsy excuse just before stepping aboard.

After they had ridden the Death Drop about three times, I worked up enough nerve to give it a try, but by then my chance had evaporated. Those kids were tired of the Death Drop and ready to try other rides. My fear of the amusement park ride's name had defeated me – even though I should have reconsidered my decision to wimp out after witnessing kid after kid exiting the ride in one piece. Instead of falling to their death, they were laughing themselves sick.

Let me pause here to clarify. Many realities should frighten you enough to turn you away in a big hurry. Drug abuse is one example. You *should* fear these wicked substances because getting hooked could ruin your health and your life. Talk about a death drop! Drugs can kill! Don't be tricked into trying to climb over the VERY REAL walls of drugs or gangs and criminal activity. You won't like what awaits on the other side!

Some high school students may face those fears. However, even more high school student share these fears: failing to graduate from high school, getting rejected by the "right" college and facing the cold shoulder of a love interest.

While one or all of these typical fears could tie up your potential, a simple formula can free it. This formula combines vision, commitment and action to use fear to your advantage – something that could make a big difference in your life and in the lives of those around you.

Vision

Weber's dictionary defines vision as "the ability to see or imagine something." Since fear is invisible, it would take Superman powers to literally detect it. Still, you can begin to overcome your fears by imagining what a fearless life would look like. Don't underestimate the power of creating this kind of vision. Every successful individual and organization began with an exciting and daring vision. Visions will show you how things can be.

Cesar Chavez had a vision for immigrant workers in the United States. He recognized that they deserved more compensation for their backbreaking farm labor, so he pushed past his fears to fight for more just conditions – something that affected thousands of people in a positive way.

Bill Gates, Martin Luther King, Jr., Steven Spielberg, the famous Williams sisters, Condoleeza Rice, and Ghandi all accomplished incredible things thanks to their extraordinary visions.

Develop your vision, and you can overcome any fear to achieve greatness!

Commitment

Once you have determined a vision for your life, you will need to give it legs – otherwise known as commitment. For instance, if your vision includes attending college, getting there will require that you buckle down and study and, later, mail the application in on time.

The bigger your commitment, the smaller your fears – those stray thoughts that question your ability to press on or follow up when you feel tired, discouraged and alone in pursuing a vision.

Commit yourself to making your dreams come true, and do not allow others to sway you!

Action

Imagining what you desire and committing yourself to getting there represent the first two steps of overcoming your fears. The third step involves taking action. In other words, GET MOVING!

Have you ever sat in a parked car? You can envision facing another direction, and you can commit to that by wrapping you fingers around the steering wheel. But until you fire up the engine and move, you won't be able to change the car's course.

A good basketball coach calls for a time out when the opposing team scores too many unanswered points. This breaks the other team's momentum. Once you decided to puncture your fears, try to keep your momentum from getting interrupted. The more ramming speed, the better chance you'll have of breaking through tissue paper walls of fear. As in basketball, it's a lot easier to keep up a winning streak when you're on a roll.

Remembering fear popping experiences will help you gain and keep this all-important momentum. For instance, I remember going to the lake to water ski with my family when I was a boy. People who saw me doubted that I could get out of the water because I have always been big – some might even call me fat. But I vividly remember bobbing neck deep in waves, holding the thin ski rope, taking a big gulp of air and then yelling *"Hit it!"* to my Dad. That's when he'd put the throttle on full tilt to blast the boat forward.

Sheer pain filled me during those first few moments of acceleration. I always figured the boat would pull my arms out of their sockets then. But once I fought through the initial shock and stood up on the skis, I couldn't believe how effortless it was to stay there! Just few seconds of discomfort gave me many minutes of fun.

As an adult, this positive childhood experience helped me build the momentum I needed to attempt stand-up comedy. I had toyed with the vision, but always got stage fright miles from the nearest comedy club. Things started changing when, just for kicks, I began introducing myself as a comedian to hear how it sounded. Next, I began picturing myself before a room full of people laughing at my jokes. I finally took action by enrolling in a comedy class and developing some original material with some big-time sweat equity.

I did a ton of rewrites and practiced my butt off. Sleep deprivation could have discouraged me during this intensive time, but my commitment to my stand-up comedian version kept me on course.

Thanks to my vision, commitment and action, I eventually stood before a full house in Hollywood at the Improv, a world renowned comedy club. I was scared silly, but I burst through that huge wall of fear with a rush of adrenaline. The crowd loved my act and laughed harder than I expected. However, with my formula in place, they could have thrown rotten tomatoes. I would have headed home, practice more and performed again.

That comedy experience taught me a valuable lesson – that fear can be your friend. It can help you rip through tissue paper walls. Once you realize how awesome getting to the other side feels, nothing you want to achieve will ever again seem impossible. You might even start looking for walls and helping others tear them down, too. That's when you can really make a difference!

Summary

Vision drives your commitment.
Commitment establishes your actions.
Action determines your life.

Vision
See yourself down the road. How will life be better for you? How will you make life better for others around you? How does success smell, taste, sound, feel and look?

Commitment
Tie yourself to your dream. Stick to it when things get rough. Ignore people who stand in your way or tell you it can't be done. Remain committed, and you'll get there sooner or later.

Action
Get going! You can dream up a great vision and commit 100 percent to it, but nothing is going to change unless you get moving.

Challenge

If fear was no obstacle, I would ______________________________

____.

What's stopping you? Don't tell me you see a wall in your way! C'mon! You *can* do it. The difference you want to make is right on the other side! Go for it!

ABOUT THE AUTHOR

Ray Lozano

A native Californian, Ray Lozano, has spoken to thousands of students during the last nineteen years. Ray has educated and entertained students in hundreds of middle schools and high schools from Alaska to Florida during his career. As a Vice Principal of a private elementary school, he launched an after-school program with an emphasis on promoting a family-oriented, drug free philosophy. Among his proudest accomplishments are participation in the creation of California's Red Ribbon Campaign and performing stand-up comedy at the Improv in Hollywood....What a great combination! Ray's life goal is to make a difference in the lives of young people and teach them to do the same in others.

Prevention Plus
841 West Marshall Blvd.
San Bernadino, CA 92405
909-855-6871
Cell: 909-855-6861
Email: RL4DFY@hotmail.com
Web Site: www.RayLozano.com

MICHAEL SCOTT KARPOVICH

The Hardest Promise to Keep

CHAPTER

15

The Hardest Promise to Keep

Michael Scott Karpovich

The Ring

Derrick Basset ran up to me after church to show me with pride – his ring. "Nice!" I said. "Know what it is?" he asked. I smiled at the young man, knowing that he had a story to tell me. "A ring?" I asked. "A promise ring!" he boasted, as if I would automatically know what that meant. I had heard of promise rings, but Derrick obviously wanted to tell me more… so I asked, "A promise ring?" "Yup," he beamed, "it is my promise to my future wife that I will save myself for her!" I mustered the most serious face I could find and looked deeply into this eighth grade boy's eyes, "Derrick, I am very proud of you, and that is a very important promise to keep!" "Yes, it is!" he exclaimed, as he turned to tell someone else about his commitment.

Was there any way that Derrick could fully understand the ramifications of the difficult promise he was making to his future bride and to himself? Not that I didn't think it was possible... I knew it was possible but certainly it is a hard promise to keep. Many years ago I made a similar commitment, and I, too, was much too young to fully understand the ramifications of my promise.

Show-And-Tell

It was a unique experience to be raised by parents like mine. Both my mother and father were scientists who left Dow Chemical Company to become full-time parents and farmers. As parents, they were very progressive. Sex was never a secret for them and even when I was very young, I was never embarrassed to ask them about it. As farmers, we would talk about which breeding stock was the best and which bull or buck we would pair off with our cattle, sheep and goats. I would then aid in the delivery of the young animals when the time came. Living on a farm, seeing and talking about sex was a very natural thing.

I don't know what prompted me, but one day I asked my parents how we, as people, should choose the "best breeding stock." Instead of laughing out loud (as perhaps some parents would have) my parents took my query very seriously. Father said, "Look for an intelligent woman like your mother." Mother said I should "look for someone who loves God." My father insisted that I should wait until I was older before I settled down. I was only in the fourth grade when my father told me I should not engage in sex until I was married. My father, not at all religious, insisted that a great marriage was based on trust. "Trust is the hardest thing to build between two people, and the easiest thing to destroy," he told me. My mother, who is very religious, insisted that God expected us to remain virgins until we got married. So

I assured my parents, when I was in the fourth grade, that I would remain a virgin until I got married.

Of course, when I announced during show-and-tell that I was a virgin, the kids laughed and I vividly remember the teacher (poor Mr. Babich) blushing and trying to quickly change the subject. Looking back, I suspect that many of my classmates really didn't understand my declaration; unfortunately, neither did ***I*** really understand. My classmates never forgot what I said in fourth grade. In fact, a year or two later, I recall Rodney, a school bully, asking if I was still a virgin. He then took it upon himself to announce to the entire class, "Karp is still a virgin!" He and one of his friends then announced that fact to our class every year, as we got older. In high school, some suggested that being a virgin meant I was less than masculine, and some just laughed at me (someone always laughed). However, I do recall a few classmates that actually seemed to respect my decision. (God bless them!)

The Hardest Part

Although I occasionally wished that I had never chosen to be so painfully honest at school about my commitment, the hardest part was never the laughter or the teasing… the hard part was HORMONES! I remember reading an article by Christian author Tim Stafford, describing hormones as a "747 Jet Engine in a Volkswagen (Beetle) Body." I still can't describe it any better! As our hormones and feelings explode, we feel like there is almost no way to resist the tide of passion sweeping over and through us.

We all want to belong, and when someone of the opposite sex expresses an interest in us, there is a piece of us that longs to know more about that person and more about ourselves. Television, magazines and friends seem to suggest that "everyone is doing it" and the few that aren't are outcasts! If you're a girl, you want a boy of your own. If you are a boy, you want a girl. It's a strong and exciting (and sometimes frightening) urge. It is hard for us to wait. There are many who don't even try. For those of us who choose to keep this promise to ourselves and our eventual spouse – it is very hard, and some of us fail.

Why Is It So Hard?

Why is sex so hard to avoid? Why can't we get it out of our minds? Why is it so very attractive? Easy answer… because we are made that way! If that is so, why does every major religion suggest that premarital (and extramarital) sex is wrong and even dangerous? Another easy answer: Because it is!

If you are in middle school, can you truly understand what it is like to be a senior? If you are in the 11th grade, can you really understand what it is like to be in college? Of course not! You may be able to make a good guess, but you don't understand until you are there. How can we possibly know what a "forever love" is like before we meet that love? We will never fully understand what marriage is like by talking to others, or reading books – the love part is *only* understood *after* the vows.

Why Are You Trying To Ruin All The Fun?

If you were to stand up in school and say you believe that sex before marriage is wrong, some might say that you are trying to ruin all the fun. "FUN?" What fun? Statistics don't lie. Millions and millions of divorces, AIDS and other STD's, adultery, abortions, unwanted pregnancies, rape, domestic violence and some pretty sick perversions all add up to a lot of pain – not fun!

Call me an unrealistic romantic, but I *do* believe in ***true love!*** I am certain that the drive within us is directing us like a compass towards that ideal person in our lives. If we don't rush into relationships because of 100% hormones but we use our reason and our values and our mind, in addition to our passion, we will find a partner, a friend and a mate who is designed for forever!

Your biology makes you want to touch, kiss, and ultimately make love. Your psychology also makes you want to touch – to love and be loved, to explore a personality so distinct from your own, to reveal your innermost thoughts and to be emotionally naked and unashamed, to never be alone again. In the meantime, you wonder if everything is right with you. Are you normal? Yes! These feelings and desires are all part of the formula – they are all part of finding that perfect love!

Find Support

Now don't go it alone. Find friends of the same sex who support your standards and who can encourage you. As I travel to speak to schools, I find that a lot more students are being bold about their sexual abstinence. You may find bold friends in your church youth group, or you may find them in your school halls... just look for people that share your values so you can have support in this promise.

If you are a runner and are going to run a marathon, you know you can't use up all your energy at the beginning of the race; you need to save it for the end. Pacing is the key. It is the same for romance. When you promise yourself that you will remain pure all the way to your wedding day, you need to pace your passion. I told every woman I ever dated that I wanted our relationship to be special – I didn't want to cheapen anything. I wanted holding hands to be sexy, our hugs to be ecstasy, and a kiss to be astounding! Because we didn't rush everything, it made our entire relationship that much more exciting! Those that rush into relationships have a hard time putting the brakes on, and if they speed too headlong into intercourse, then hand holding loses all of its meaning!

Why Wait?

Is it worth the wait? Of course! The new car is exciting because it is new to you; graduation is that much more exciting because it is something we have to work towards; the buried treasure becomes more of a treasure because it is buried.

What if two people are desperately in love? What if they are absolutely certain they'll marry someday? That is absolutely great! This is the time when you engage the mind; this is when you talk about what this promise really means to both of you; and these are the moments when you expand the meaning of the ***friendship*** part of your life! When you ***do*** marry, it will be for more than just love. It will be a promise of forever – a lifelong commitment! You only get one "first time" in your life and there is great joy in sharing it with your forever love.

People who choose to have intercourse without this total commitment and total friendship will find it difficult to ever understand what total surrender to another person is all about. If sex simply means "I think you are attractive" or "You make me hot" – it will be very hard to change your mind into thinking "You are my all, and I give myself exclusively to you!"

Wedding night jitters…of course you will be nervous! But that is the exciting part of the most important night of your life. Virgins are uniquely able to give their whole selves to love in marriage. "The first time" *must* be a big deal – you are giving your total self to the one great love of your life. At that moment you will both dive into mysteries you have wondered about most of your life – and you will explore those mysteries with the one person you love more than any other! It is like bungee jumping, skydiving, and a huge celebration all wrapped into one! For those who are sexually promiscuous, a honeymoon is simply a nice vacation.

Proud To Be A Virgin!

As I mentioned earlier, when my peers laughed at me and called me "Preacher Karp," "Virgin," or "Queer," it was uncomfortable, but a part of me (deep inside) made me that much more resolved to keep my promise. I faced a lot of temptation in high school, a hundred times more in college, and even more after I graduated from the University. Now I travel to high schools across North America and occasionally I am asked to speak about the choice of abstinence. Of course, I have a unique story… I have waited longer than most men. When I tell people I am proud to be a virgin, I don't get the laughter that I have come to expect; instead, I have been getting applause – even standing ovations!

I genuinely believe that students are *hungry* to hear that someone can "be cool" and make the choice of abstinence. In the past few years, more rock stars, musicians, actors, and athletes have taken the bold stance to say they have chosen to wait for love.

Make A Difference

Since this book is about making a difference, you may be asking yourself how you can make a difference in such a personal area. Well, first of all, you are making a ***very big*** difference in ***your*** life if you make this decision for yourself. Second, if you are very brave, you can share your decision with your friends and other students at school. We need to let people know that, in reality, there are a lot of students that have made the decision to wait for marriage, so that people won't feel the unrealistic peer pressure that "everyone else is doing it" and will have the courage to stand firm in their decision. And that can make a ***very big*** difference in a ***lot*** of people's lives!

My Forever Love

After a long romantic relationship, I finally married the one and only woman for me! I am so in love! She is my best friend and more… and we are both overjoyed that we have waited. Our relationship is so deep; it is so spiritual – we are so meaningful together. Students come up to me after my talk and thank me for telling them about my choice. I have had lots of athletes, scholars, artists and tough kids tell me that they will join me in keeping that same promise to themselves. I have had dozens of kids pull me aside and admit that although they have had sex in the past, they have made the decision to not have sex again until they get married (which is so amazingly cool)!

By the time you pick up this book I will have been married for months, maybe a year. In fact, as I write this chapter, I am just back from my honeymoon. (Actually, I tell my beloved that this honeymoon will never end!) Keep the promise for your perfect love and for yourself. And I can tell you, from this side of "the hardest promise to keep," it is well worth it!

ABOUT THE AUTHOR

Michael Scott Karpovich, CSP

... practices what he preaches! A newlywed, Michael says that waiting until marriage to give the gift of yourself is the greatest gift of all! Despite a difficult start, Michael's faith in Christ and his life experiences have made him into what he calls a "blessed nerd!" Diagnosed with "brain damage" at age four, beaten up by bullies, and severely dyslexic, Michael has discovered strength comes from weathering challenges. As he puts it... "Yuk makes you stronger!" Michael speaks at high schools and leadership conferences about how to stand up for what you believe in, how to make a difference in the world, and how to be resilient!

Michael Scott Karpovich, CSP
The Meeting Partner
P.O. Box 272
Caro, MI 48723-0272
989-673-3036 Fax: 801-459-4696
Toll Free: 1-800-718-3367
Email: info@Karpovich.com
Web Site: www.TheHighSchoolSpeaker.com

Outro-duction

You made it to the end of the book and what did you find?

You discovered that in today's world, you have two choices: to get mad or to **GO MAD!**

It's easy to sit on the sidelines and be a critic of the game. It takes no skill – and no sacrifice – to complain, to rant, and to condemn. The challenge comes only when you decide to get off your butt and get on the field; to play your heart out in an attempt to live life fully and to make a difference in the lives of others.

We have called you out of the crowd and dared you to get on the field of play.

We've challenged and empowered you to raise your hand high in the air and scream, "Pick Me!" And we know that you have made the right choice.

You have chosen to be "it." You are going to get involved. You are going to stand up for all that is right. You are going to give until it hurts, and then you are going to give some more.

It feels good to be "it" – doesn't it? In fact, the only thing that feels better is *tagging* other people. Creating more "its." Knowing that others have been infected by your GO MAD virus and that they are now out spreading goodwill and good deeds.

So in the spirit of love and empowerment, **GO MAD** and play tag!

MADdening Ideas

Part One

Real Stuff You Can Do That is Sure to Make a Difference Around Your School

Go M.A.D. Bulletin Board

When asked why they are not more involved in service-oriented projects, most students respond that they are unaware of scheduled activities or who to contact. To alleviate that, create a bulletin board in your school that clearly lists special upcoming projects and events along with contact information. Also, provide a drop box for students and faculty members to submit ideas for future projects.

Friday "Food for Thought"

Schedule a different school club or team to host a Friday "Thank you" snack table at the central teachers' lounge or front office. That group can spread that table with bagels or other goodies along with coffee, cookies and milk to give back and give thanks to those underpaid and underappreciated adults who make a difference. Don't forget to welcome the cooks, custodial staff and front office personnel to the table as well!

Secret Samaritan Wish Box

Using the idea behind the various "Make A Wish" organizations, set up a drop box where students can submit special wishes or requests for other students or faculty members who may need a lift. Then, start a club of student "wish grantors," those interested in working together to do nice things for needy people.

Go M.A.D. Week

Your school has a homecoming or spirit week, so why not coordinate a special week that encourages service project involvement? Each day, focus on a different cause to inform students and motivate them to get involved. For example, the week could include Feed the Hungry Monday, Stop AIDS Tuesday, etc. On Friday, hold an all-school assembly to celebrate student good deeds and to recognize those who have truly gone the extra mile to make a difference.

Penny for Your Thoughts

Plan and promote a special day on your campus to recognize people who have made a difference by handing them a penny. Naturally, the penny only serves as the day's designated symbol – a token that reminds the student to verbalize their appreciation and gratitude as they hand it over. This is a day that really makes *cents.*

Public Displays of Affection

Reserve an easily accessible area at school with a bulletin board or display case. Use this space to post public notes of appreciation. Use a drop box to collect notes and select new ones to display each week.

Service with a Smile

Assemble a group of your peers and secretly select one school day to spoil each faculty member. As the teachers pull into their parking spots before classes begin, your group could go to the designated teacher to cheer, open the car door and usher him or her into school to be met by rousing applause from other students. From there, another student group could escort that teacher into the classroom while carrying his or her books and briefcase. Finally, bring the designated teacher coffee and a bagel along with a certificate of appreciation. Can you think of a better way for a teacher to start the day?

Dime a Dozen

For two weeks straight, collect a dime each day from the students in your homeroom. At the end of this period, you will have collected $1.00 from each student. With that $20 to $30, purchase a nice plant for your teacher's room. If the room has no windows, buy a cactus or some low-light potted plant. Try to keep your mission a secret in order to surprise your teacher.

Colorful Collaboration Experiment

To eliminate cliques and celebrate diversity, plan a surprise day to mix things up. Ask your principal make an announcement at the end of the day asking all students to come to school the next morning wearing a solid-colored shirt. The next day, the principal's a morning announcement would state that students can only associate with other students wearing the same color of shirt. This will encourage interaction between people that don't typically associate, and in this way can be a springboard for discussions on prejudice and diversity.

Pay it Forward *with Class*

As a class, get your teacher's approval to schedule a day to surprise the class next door with cookies and milk. Do this for no other reason than to spread good will. Encourage the class receiving the mini-party to repay the favor, but not toward your class. Watch as they plan to outdo your efforts by doing something nice – and unsuspecting – for another class down the hall. You might see a chain reaction where your original act of kindness makes its way through the entire campus, perhaps even back to your class!

Locker Recognition

Ask each teacher to anonymously select and submit the names of two or three students who have either done well at a particular project or showed some real improvement or helped another in a special way. Then, form a group to surprise these students by decorating their lockers with congratulatory signs, posters, streamers and balloons. Make certain each recipient knows the specific reasons that they are being honored.

MADdening Ideas

Part Two

Real Stuff You Can Do That is Sure to Make a Difference Around Your Community

Fall Clean-up for Senior Citizens

In cooler climates, preparing for winter is a demanding job for anyone. But raking leaves, changing storm windows, storing lawn furniture, etc. are even more difficult for the elderly. To help out local seniors, organize a fall clean-up crew. Then, place an announcement in the local newspaper listing the name and telephone number needed to schedule a work crew visit. By spending a few weekends moving from house to house, you will help some very needy folks.

"Pile of Warmth" Coat Drive

Look through your closets, and you'll find a few coats you probably haven't put on since dinosaurs walked the earth. Why not get them in the hands of the needy? Start a pile of warmth with your coats, and get your family to give you theirs. Then, call on your neighbors and friends. Before long, you'll have a humongous pile. To hand it over, contact your local rescue mission for homeless people to schedule a drop off time.

"Double the Difference" Trash-a-thon

In the same way you drum up donations for a bowl-a-thon or a walk-a-thon, ask individuals and local businesses to sponsor you and your friends in picking up trash along a littered street, highway or greenbelt. Charge sponsors on a per hefty bag basis – for instance, $1 per bag. Then, donate proceeds to another charity to get a double-the-difference impact by helping two causes with one event!

Senior Prom

You're never too old to party, but social activities for the elderly tend to seem dull and mundane. Spice things up for senior citizens in your area by throwing a prom just for them. Decorate your school's gymnasium or cafeteria to reflect the way it might have looked at a dance 40 to 50 years ago. Collect some old big band recordings for the DJ to spin or use your own sound system. Provide refreshments. Finally, arrange for school buses to transport seniors to and from their nursing homes and senior centers, and you've got the makings of a real shindig that they will never forget!

Junior Prom

Similar to the senior prom idea, sponsor a party for local elementary school students. Recruit friends to chaperone and lead games, group dances and other activities for the younger kids. This will give you an opportunity to role model exceptional social behavior and manners while helping them have a great time.

Safe Ride Hotline

Assemble a student team to help peers get home safely from a party or date where they feel uncomfortable or unsafe. To this end, establish a no-questions-asked hotline that will ring to a cell phone manned by team members trained in arranging quick and safe transportation for the distressed caller. This hotline can be set up for high-risk situations such as prom and graduation night or on weekends throughout the school year if needed.

Mile of Quarters

Inform the student body that you are collecting a "mile of quarters" for a needy charity. Find a local florist willing to donate a mile of ribbon in your school colors, making certain that the ribbon is a minimum of four inches wide so that four quarters can be laid down side-by-side. Give this promotion a solid month, but occasionally roll out the ribbon across a gymnasium floor or football field to demonstrate the progress. The excitement among your classmates, teachers, and parents will build as more and more people get involved collecting quarters for the cause. Once the ribbon stretches a full mile, you will have raised $10,000!

Little Champions

This project allows underprivileged or low-income children in your community to more fully experience the joy of sports. Contact the recreation centers and community athletic programs geared to this group to determine what equipment needs to be supplied or replaced. Then, coordinate a new and used sporting goods drive through local churches and schools to collect baseball gloves, bats, balls, cleats, skates, helmets, etc.

Books-R-Us

Invite your community to donate new and used books in good condition to children living in low-income areas. Invite area bookstores to contribute, too. After the book drive, round up volunteers and vehicles to deliver the books door to door. Encourage these delivery people to read a story or two to the children before leaving.

Hospital Cheer for Tots

Hospitals are scary places for kids. Brighten their day by visiting with balloons, streamers, dollar store trinkets and smiles to wish them a happy "non-birthday." Also, make up funny "Happy Non-birthday" lyrics and sing them with gusto. In these ways, you can transform part of an unfortunate hospital stay into something pleasantly memorable.

Tip Included with Service

At a fast food drive thru, give a complimentary window wash to customers waiting for orders. After wiping their windshield, you can share a quick tip about youth, such as "Kids are less likely to do drugs if their parents and relatives talk to them about the dangers of drugs" or "Let's leave a clean world to our children. Recycle every chance you get." This is a great way to share a message you feel passionately about in a friendly, unique way.

Adopt-an-Adult

Adopt a senior citizen, disabled person or anyone else who may need assistance and establish a time to drop by weekly to pick up some of their chores – yard work, trash removal, snow shoveling, etc. Challenge others at your school, both individuals and clubs, to participate as well. Later, plan social events to swap heartwarming stories and photos of your experiences.

Reverse Protest

Angry citizens typically assemble to hold signs, chant and protest wars and other issues. Shock your community – and the media – by rallying friends to trumpet a message of thanks to parents, police, teachers and others for all they do to make the community a better place.

Wheelchair Drive

You'd be surprised at how many people with disabilities need wheelchairs, but cannot afford them. Organize a scavenger hunt throughout your community to find unused wheelchairs, and then donate them to organizations in touch with those in need.

Shoes for the Shoeless

Organize a shoe drive at your school and neighborhood. Use masking tape to keep each pair together, and then write the correct size of each pair on the tape before delivering the used shoes to a rescue mission or homeless shelter.

Write a Letter

Do you feel passionately about a certain issue? Write to your congressional or state representatives and senators, your mayor and other leaders to express your thoughts and opinions. Calls and e-mails can also be effective, but snail mail gets into the public record. For more impact, get your friends and family to write similar letters to the same officials. This is an exceptional way to get your voice heard by someone with the power to take action.

Make Sure to Get Every Book in the TEEN POWER Series!

For High School & College Students

Christ-Centered Stories

For Middle Schoolers

For Parents & Teachers

Visit us on the web at
www.teenpower.com